Praise for the Fir

M000041340

"Donna's book is filled with guidance for maximizing our potential for spiritual growth and planetary transformation. What a testimony to the sufficiency of the indwelling spirit of God for revealing our purpose, meaning, and true self! This is a book to be read, reread, and incorporated into one's life adventure."

—Rosemarie Stallworth-Clark, PhD, Professor Emerita, Georgia Southern University

"I first came to Donna's book not long after beginning my own journey into the practice of stillness meditation. Donna's book showed me how to center my stillness practice on cultivating my relationship with God. What I find remarkable is that—while her approach is systematic and comprehensive, and therefore intellectually satisfying—it is also warm and personal, and thereby gratifying spiritually. I have adapted several of the practices Donna offers in this book into classroom exercises for helping teenagers find inner grounding in these turbulent times."

—John Creger, award-winning high school English teacher

The wisdom in *Teach Us to Love* gracefully details the age-less way to self-discovery, inner peace, and spiritual growth. The book is an elegant, inspiring guide to personal transformation – the essential element for world transformation. The truth so beautifully shared here provides the sustainable foundation that humanity needs to create the enlightened world we all want."

—John Otranto, Commander, U.S. Coast Guard, Retired

"A wonderful guide for any person seeking to advance on their spiritual path and to deepen their relationship with God. Especially helpful is the chapter on spiritual, emotional, and physical healing that leads to a balanced life."

— *Dolores Nice, retired school administrator*

"We are a world of people who have not been loved enough. Many of us acknowledge that God loves us, but this is a mere shadow of being enlivened by a love that cleanses and then empowers us to live as children of God. Donna helps us to realize that our innocent need for unconditional love has been thwarted generation after generation, burdening us with an unworthiness that keeps our hearts from opening fully to the flow of Divine love. And skillfully, with great tenderness she shows us how to do just that."

— *Deborah Goaldman, junior high school teacher*

"Donna shows us how to grasp the fuller meaning of love, and be transformed in the process."

— *Leoma Sparer*

"In this book, Donna D'Ingillo illuminates the way for you to create a personal and dynamic relationship to Spirit. If you are on a spiritual journey to heal your life and live in love, forgiveness, and understanding, this book is a must-read."

— *Sandra L. Porter*

Teachings for the child of God in each of us

Teach Us to Love

Finding Unconditional Love
through Communion with God

Donna D'Ingillo

Origin Press
Celestia

To Gretchen ~
many your blossom
in God's love & peace
and be filled with
joy!.
love,
Donna

Celestia
An imprint of Origin Press

PO Box 151117 • San Rafael, CA 94915
www.originpress.com

Cover design by William Hays
william@theartistsloft.com

Author photo by Kate Weaver
kate@kateweaver.com
Kate Weaver Portrait Photography, Inc.

ISBN 978-193-1254182

To order additional copies of the book, contact:
Center for Christ Consciousness
www.ctrforchristcon.org

First published in 2002
New edition 2011

Printed in the United States of America

DEDICATION

Dedicated to the glory of God, in loving service to
Christ Michael (Jesus), for the edification of humanity.

ACKNOWLEDGEMENTS

Over the years of writing this book, there have been many people who supported me with their love, encouragement and guidance, most notably Mary Boyden, Mark Hall, Sally Martin, Mark Moore, David Painter, and Connie Withers.

Special appreciation and acknowledgement is also due to the members of the Stillness Foundation Board of Directors: Michael Painter, Marty Risacher, Sandy Porter, Mark Hall, and Jim Cleveland.

My deepest gratitude also to my friend Carlotta for her superlative editing contribution; to Byron Belitsos for his heroic publishing efforts; and to Peter Hayman, Jacques Lecouturier, and Lynn Goodwin for also helping to make this book a reality; to my parents, Guy and Charlotte D'Ingillo (now on their ascension careers) for their love and support; and finally, to the spiritual support of my unseen spiritual helpers, without whose guidance and love this book would never have been possible.

TABLE OF CONTENTS

INTRODUCTION

Section I:
YOUR RELATIONSHIP
WITH GOD

Section II:
SPIRITUAL ATTITUDES AND HABITS

Section III:
THE FAITH ADVENTURE

Section IV:
FINALE

INTRODUCTION

Author's Preface

Have you ever considered what your life would be like if you felt truly loved in the depths of your being? How would such an experience of profound love change you?

I pondered this question for a long time, and it has formed the basis of my search to find such love deep in my own heart. And yet, when I looked at my own relationships with myself or with others, or the relationships between people I know, too often I discovered the same phenomenon: Virtually none of us receives due recognition in our primary relationships of who we really are. Our primal essence is not being validated; we simply are not being loved. And this is the case even though we all know that unconditional love – total acceptance of who we are as individuals – is a fundamental human need.

As social creatures, we have within us a driving force that propels us into interactions with others. Our connections with them are often based on the various roles we choose to take on, yet the common denominator in all of our relationships is the universal desire to be understood, accepted, respected, and loved. As we seek to fulfill these needs, we tend to overlook the most obvious place in which to find the love we crave – within ourselves. We look to our spouses, our children, our friends, our colleagues, to fill that void, placing great demands on our significant others. But sooner or later, some lack of acceptance, understanding, and love is bound to creep into our interactions, and our expectations meet with disappointment.

In all human relationships, there will always be a dream that fails; some needs will always remain unfulfilled. But having unrealistic expectations of others in the first place is the problem. The hurt feelings, mistrust, and anger that can flare up when we feel misundertstood, abandoned, or outright rejected are the inevitable results of demanding what is beyond another's capacity to give. How can someone else know who you really are? How can an imperfect human being fully or perfectly understand what is in your heart and mind? How can another person see the world from your perspective when they have their own way of seeing and thinking? How can you expect love and acceptance from others who struggle with their own lack of self-love and acceptance?

If in fact we cannot get all of what we need from others, then there must be some other source to fulfill our basic desire for love. But what is that source, and how do we find it?

By definition, love exists only within personal relationships – it is never a mere abstraction. This book, and my own experience, shows that a perfect source of love can only be found in a perfect personality: God, who is the source of all love.

Teach Us to Love is a spiritual manual that describes who and what this divine source of love is and how to develop a personal relationship with God. Its basic teaching is simple: Each of us can find the love we are seeking by setting aside a time each day to go within and make contact with the Spirit of God that dwells within our higher consciousness. This internal presence is the gateway to divinity and deity, our connection to a higher dimension of universe reality— the realm of Spirit itself.

We have direct access to this higher dimension through the practices of stillness, prayer, worship, and service as described in this book. In other words, when we pass through this portal, we find the love that fulfills our core need. Once this primal need is satisfied, we are ready to focus our attention on developing our innate gifts and talents as we learn how to be increasingly inspiring and helpful to one another and to our planet as a whole.

A Personal Introduction:

Finding the Perfect Love

I am most fortunate that my quest for perfect love has led me on a rewarding spiritual journey over the course of my life. My search began early on, for even as a young child, I naturally expected to receive unconditional love from within my family. But the needs of my sensitive and emotional nature were too big for my parents and siblings to fill. As I grew into adolescence and early womanhood, I looked outward to find fulfilling love from young men, but once again I was disappointed. Throughout these early life lessons, all I ever really wanted was to feel loved, deep in my being. Not feeling this love was a constant source of frustration and confusion; indeed, even my marriage did not give me the deep sense of being cherished that I craved.

Only much later did an event occur that led me to go within—into that sacred place in the quietude of my heart—to that inner realm in which I began to truly feel loved and valued. There I found the love I had been looking for all of my life, the love that changed and healed me—a love that set me free to explore who I am. The door of my heart finally opened to God, and it was then that I began a spiritual journey that has brought me tremendous peace of mind. I had discovered the perfect love that God shares with me as a child of Spirit! And it is the task of this book to inspire you to make a similar journey.

Receiving the Lessons of
a Celestial Teacher

The basic spiritual instruction provided in *Teach Us to Love* is offered by celestial personalities—unseen personalities with whom I have contact. Their chief delight is to help us awaken to the spirit realm through lessons about who we are as beloved children of a divine Creator. It is they who provide tools for our transformation as they "teach us to love." I did not always know about these wonderful beings; the story of their entry into my life completely changed my understanding of what love is and how I could learn how to love myself and others.

Being a rather sensitive child, I had a strong intuitive hunger for God. These pangs of truth-hunger remained in me throughout my youth, even though I was raised in a traditional Christian church, attending it regularly and reading the Bible. Then, in 1975 – when I was just twenty-one – I was very fortunate to find an amazing revelatory book of truth, *The Urantia Book*, that satisfied my intellectual hunger for God. Yet even this gift of revelation did not fill me with the love I craved deep in my heart.

But all that changed in 1992 when, as a member of a group of **Urantia Book** readers, a new kind of grace entered my life: Our group suddenly began to receive lessons transmitted to us by an unseen celestial teacher. This invisible being spoke through various group members, including me, in weekly "transmissions." We were thrilled as he began to provide us with valuable and practical instruction on growing spiritually, healing our emotions, and making contact with that still small voice of God within.

Our celestial teacher explained to us that our world is currently in the very early stages of a massive shift in consciousness. As one part of that mission of planetary uplift—which he called the Teaching Mission—he provided profound lessons about who we are as humans living on our planet, our place in the universe, and who and what God is. He also explained that a large host of celestial helpers had been dispatched to Earth to help individuals and groups like ours learn to love one another and recognize our innate value as children of a loving divine Creator.

In this new worldwide mission initiated by our unseen celestial friends, the basic practice recommended for everyone centers on what the teachers call the practice of stillness. To practice stillness, we were told, we should set aside a time to remove ourselves from the busyness of the day, and then quiet our mind in order to perceive the voice of God that lives within our higher consciousness. In that place of rest, they said, we would discover all of the spiritual answers that we would ever need; here we would actually experience God's love for us.

My daily effort of engaging in this simple practice with the help of our celestial teacher led me to find the love I had sought all of my life. In fact, the practice of stilling my mind and making contact with the Spirit of God within me was so successful that it healed parts of me that I did not even know were wounded. Stillness practice took me into an inner realm where I was able to understand who I am as a child of God. It even led me to discover my life's purpose.

Our superhuman teacher had much more to share with us. He opened the door to an understanding of this unique time in our planet's history, a new era in which the heavenly realms are converging upon Earth for our spiritual upliftment.

The Advent of the Correcting Time

As time went on, we learned that our world is presently experiencing what is known as the "Correcting Time," a new phase of planetary history that has been intiated to bring humans to the realization that they are members of a cosmic family – the family of God.

Now that the Correcting Time has been inaugurated, the dormant spiritual potential in humanity is being stimulated as never before. Through the power of this "spiritual pressure from above," we are able to get beyond mere belief systems and dogma to perceive God as both a spirit person and the energy force of love. Ultimately, it is in developing a personal relationship with God that we will find the perfect love we seek.

Each individual on this world is, in reality, a beloved child of God. Each individual is worthy and deserving of God's unconditional love just because he or she exists. This time of correction is designed to help each person come to this realization: that all are worthy children of God, and that each one of us has the God-given privilege and right to be loved.

The many lessons of the Correcting Time inspire us to share and spread love by first teaching us to love ourselves, and then to learn how to love others. When people feel and act out of love, they naturally exude the fruits of the spirit: patience, tolerance, goodwill, peace, compassion, understanding, kindness, and joy. And when enough of us demonstrate this behavior, a new spiritual momentum will overtake the world and heal our planet of all its sorrows. The current era in which we are now living is a time of great healing, both for our planet as well as for ourselves.

Of course, it would be wonderful if this world could be miraculously transformed into a utopia where love is dominant and pervasive. But planetary transformation is an evolving phenomenon that will come about only through the gradual transformation of individuals who dare, one by one, to cast aside the surrounding ills of our inherited culture with its profound errors in thinking. Only those individuals who courageously strive to live their lives in dedication to the ideals of spiritual reality – inspired by truth, motivated by goodness, and reflective of beauty – will be able to change the culture.

The upshot is that the greater universe is sending us new spiritual influences along with a corps of extradimensional teachers. A brilliant new epoch is now dawning. We are continuously being helped to more deeply experience the love that God shares with us as we build the ways of heaven on Earth.

In essence, the Correcting Time encourages all the peoples of our world to seek spiritual growth as a goal of living – but each in their own way. In fact, messages similar to those our group has received can now be found in many places, and those lessons are designed to uplift and inspire people all over the planet in accord with the terms and symbols of their own religious and spiritual traditions. This is indeed a time when the hearts and minds of all the inhabitants of this world are waking to the call of spirit, regardless of their religious beliefs, since truth transcends all of man's religious, secular, and philosophical belief systems. No one religion has cornered the market on truth. Wherever people are willing to learn new spiritual principles and values, wherever people are willing to discard hate and prejudice, wherever people embrace love and goodness, unseen celestial and angelic help is now available like never before to guide them in their journey to enlightenment.

It is worth emphasizing that the spiritual transformation of our world is an evolutionary process that will take many, many years to accomplish. It will not occur overnight or even in one generation. There is no miracle cure. There is no shortcut, no quick fix. And it must happen individual by individual.

But where you see love in action, God's presence is there. Where you see people once separated by racial prejudice coming together in tolerance and understanding, Spirit is there. Where you see communities healing their wounds of poverty, ignorance, and hate, God's love is there. Where you see the values of truth, beauty, and goodness living in the lives of people striving to lead decent, compassionate lives, God is there. And wherever you see people coming together in harmony, peace, understanding and love, Spirit is there as well.

It is clear that many pathways are now available for bringing about the unique planetary upliftment known as the Correcting Time. The truth of the family of God can be expressed in innumerable ways because each person is a matchless expression of God's love. The way is open to everyone, and each person is free to experience God in his or her own way.

Developing a Personal Relationship with God

One of the key distinctions our celestial teacher shared with our group concerned the centrality of the personal aspect of God. We have the capacity to perceive divnity in several distinct ways – for example, as an energy force, or as the principle of universal love. Yet it is only by developing a personal relationship with a personal God that we truly experience that sublime and perfect love that God delights in sharing with us as children of Spirit. This is because – as our teacher explained over and over – love exists only in personal relationships; you cannot receive love from a thing or force. This notion may at first sound counterintuitive; for example, many people report feeling great love just from being in nature, or with a pet. But whenever you experience love in any form, its source is this personal face of God. This is true even if one doesn't believe in God as a Spirit person.

Our limited understanding of who and what God is may color and condition our perception of the nature of God, but from the divine perspective, the limitations in our human perceptions do not ultimately matter. God understands why we have so many beliefs about the spiritual nature of reality and the beingness of Spirit. He accepts all sincere human approaches to deity.

After explaining this, our teacher then went on to propose this notion: How could any human know you better than the divine Creator? How could anyone possibly understand more than the One in whom all things exist? Because God created you, no one else can know you as completely. God knows you better than you know yourself. God knows everything about you.

But do you know God? God loves you dearly, but do you love God? Do you really feel love for your Creator? Knowing God is more than just thinking about the Divine One. It is more than an intellectual exercise. You may believe that God exists in various ways, but to feel God's love alive inside you is something entirely different. It is more than a belief; it is an awareness of a dynamic presence deep inside your being. The knowledge of God resides in the mind, but the experience of God flourishes in your heart.

If you truly want to feel the deepest love possible, the personal approach to God affords you the satisfaction that your heart yearns for. But how would you do this?

It is actually simpler than you might think. Getting acquainted with God is no different than getting to know any other person. How do you get to truly know someone? You become familiar with him or her by spending time together. The same principle applies to becoming acquainted with God: You enjoy time with God in order to develop a relationship. *Teach Us to Love* offers you many ways to spend time with God by guiding you to develop a truly personal relationship so that you can live a fuller, more joy-filled life. Your life can be rich with love.

Feeling God's unconditional love elevates the intellectual belief in God to a much higher level – to a spiritual level. It transcends our limiting beliefs about God, leading us to faith in God. And spiritual living does not mean that you have to be perfect or give up material pleasures. Spiritual living is nothing more than being aware of and striving to gain godly ideals. It means progressively attuning yourself to those ideals and values that enable you to love and understand yourself more fully, recognize your life purpose, and love others. In this process, your sense of self-worth blooms like a flower opening in the sunlight. Your personality blossoms, basking in the illumination of God's love. You become the person you were born to be. Your life unfolds to your soul's satisfaction. Your innermost yearnings become fulfilled. Your capacity for happiness, peace, and love increases immeasurably. Your heart is filled with joy!

My Experience with the Teachings

After being on the receiving end of these lessons for the past eighteen years, I can truly say that life has become more fulfilled. I have been able to overcome the wounds of my past. I've learned to face my fears and mistakes, and put them in a new perspective. This has freed me from their negative hold and has changed my feelings and behavior. As a child, I experienced a repression of my true nature at the hands of my family, friends, and the belief systems that an immature youngster develops. This was played out in my life in later years in the form of deep anger, guilt, and resentment. Through the experience of feeling God's powerful love, I no longer feel ruled by these emotions. This is not to say that I never feel destructive emotions anymore. However, I find that they arise significantly less frequently and dissolve more easily than before I started to practice the stillness and develop my love connection with God. And I am able to release myself from their grip before they affect another person negatively.

For much of my life, I felt that I was unworthy and unacceptable to God. I would look in the mirror and see a fraud that no one could love. And while my rational mind knew this was ridiculous, my emotional self felt otherwise. But God's love has great healing power, and I no longer feel the guilt of imperfection nagging at me. Instead, I have found that seeking God's loving guidance gives me the opportunity to make those decisions that help me to do things positively.

In addition, I no longer feel that I have offended God by my mistakes. I do not feel cut off from unconditional love because of my past behavior or errors in judgment. Now, even though I still make mistakes like anyone else, I know God loves me despite my foolish, imperfect actions. He does not expect me to be perfect – just to turn to Spirit for help and support. This understanding has given me a tremendous sense of freedom and a lightheartedness. The more I trust God, the more my joy and levity about life increases!

I feel peaceful most of the time now, and more importantly, I feel loved. I know who I am and what I want to do with my life. My self-esteem, confidence, and personal creativity are at levels I have never before experienced. I have moved to a new career that is more satisfying to the "me" I wish to become. My future is bright and full of hope. This is in stark contrast to the past when I would take the safe jobs that afforded financial security but little personal creative expression. Now embarked on a new path, I find that I am being led to those opportunities that keep me afloat financially and that allow me the freedom to express myself. I have the best of both worlds.

My physical health has also improved through this practice, because I spend time each day connecting to the feelings of peace and well-being that God lavishes on me. This has diminished my feelings of stress and being out of control, which translates into a healthier immune system that is more resistant to disease and cell degeneration. I feel alive, vital, and energized!

I also find that I have developed more patience, compassion, and tolerance for others. In the past, I noticed that I often would not listen to or respect what other people had to say. I would not honor their God-given right to their own opinion. How arrogant of me! I am happy to say that this attitude toward others has improved. I also feel more generous and forgiving when others hurt me, and I do my best to understand the inner pain that makes them act unkindly. I honor their path.

I feel the deep love God has for me. The care, understanding, and compassion He gives me during my instruction is real, it is palpable. Along with this, He also teaches me about other places and realities in the universe. He shows me how different life is from how we know it to be here on this planet. There is so much more evil, so much hate, so much more negativity on this world than on other worlds and dimensions. As I feel His love more and more fully, I am beginning to taste the incredible love waiting for us out there in the great spiritual beyond. The universe is truly good.

The security of love and the assurance that I am a beloved child of a great and loving divine Parent have given me boundless joy. And these are not just mere words; they are a living dynamic force within me. Such experiences are the only real proof of the validity of these teachings, which is found in the personal experience and feelings of greater peace and happiness.

Finally, I have uncovered the great truth that love, goodness, mercy, and justice truly do reign supreme in the universe. This is of great comfort to me. The living truth that we are all made to experience God's love and to love one another has given me the greatest satisfaction and the most happiness I have ever experienced. It truly has healed me and made me a whole, happy, and growing person. And I can honestly say that this can easily happen to you, too, if you are willing to walk this path.

Experiencing the Lessons in this Book

We are given much help from Spirit as we learn how to live more satisfying lives. Yet many times we close ourselves off to our spirituality because our culture does not value it as an approach to successful living, or perhaps because we do not understand how to bring it into our daily lives. We often turn to external religious or social institutions for answers and look to "experts" for answers. The messages in this book will help you readjust your thinking and instead look inside yourself for the answers, for the true wisdom.

What follows is a compilation and restatement of the concepts that I have learned over many years concerning how to develop a personal relationship with God and feel Spirit's loving and healing presence. These teachings have been culled from several years of direct instruction from our original celestial teacher. They offer basic truths, but please bear in mind that you will encounter much greater depth of meaning and understanding as you grow in experience and wisdom.

Some of these ideas may be quite new to you; some may even be startling or challenge beliefs you have held for your whole life. What I have discovered is that our preconceived ideas often blind us to hidden jewels of truth and cause us to discard unfamiliar answers to our questions. Too many times, we go along with a popularly held notion only because it is generally accepted; we never question its validity. But analyzing ideas at a superficial, intellectual level does not reveal their true meanings. Inner knowing is different than believing in ideas. Truth is best assessed at a heartfelt, instinctive, gut level. When you are confronted with spiritual or religious teachings of any kind, this intuitive nature helps you to gauge whether the answers are valid. You feel it inside your being. It goes right to your heart. When you accept something as true, an inner light should go on in your mind that tells you, "This is right, this is correct." This inner truth sensor is a divine gift.

So as you read this book, I ask you to consider the content of this material and see for yourself whether or not it appeals to your inner sense of truth. I suggest that you ask yourself the following questions to determine whether the specific ideas it contains are true for you: Does this message make me feel good about myself? Do I feel closer to God? Does it make me a happier and more loving person? Will it help me get along better with others? Do I feel loved as I read the words? Is the message positive? Do I feel more love and tolerance for others?

I consider myself a seeker of truth, and because I feel that what has been revealed to me is true, my wish is to share it with you. But you must decide whether these messages ring true for you. Assess the content, experience the message, and observe how you are changed by it. If you feel more uplifted about life after reading this book, and if you sense that this book has indeed taught you to love, then it has served its purpose.

Donna D'Ingillo
August 20, 2010

Section I:

YOUR RELATIONSHIP WITH GOD

The foundation of spiritual growth is built upon the basics: The heart of learning to love yourself and others is to begin with the source of all love, the source of all creation – God, our Creator-Parent. Nothing less than beginning with God will give the broad perspective on who you are and where you are going. God is the planner, initiator, and controller of life. God is the source of love that propels life into action. Nothing happens without Spirit's plan and action, and no person or thing can ever live without the existence of God, the Divine First Source and Center.

1

God's Approach to Humans

Who Is God?

First and foremost, God is a creator who has a special intimate and loving relationship with those He creates. God is the Universal Parent to His creation, and all His children. Therefore, think of God as a Divine Parent, the Universal Father/Mother. While God transcends all gender barriers, God has a personality with whom you can relate — God is detectable. It is most important to envisage God as having a personal relationship with you as an individual.

From the human standpoint, it is helpful to relate to God as if Spirit were a person rather than an impersonal force or energy presence. You relate to a person easier than you can to something impersonal, for it is people with whom you have meaningful relationships. Whether you personally use the term "Father," "Mother," "God," "Spirit," or any other term, or even if your training leads you to conceive of God as a great presence/force, envisioning yourself communicating with God in a personal relationship cultivates the opportunity for you to know God as a loving personality. When approaching the spiritual connection you wish to deepen, it is helpful to not allow human gender meanings or human religious concepts of God to overshadow the truth of our Divine Creator, for Spirit's presence and being encompasses all reality. What is important is to see yourself having a relationship with God, however you choose to depict this Supreme Being of creation.

The Universal Father/Mother creates many levels of personalities as an expression of love and sharing. It is God's desire to share the grand universe of Spirit's making with all creation. The universe is the domicile of God's children, and all of Spirit's blessings are freely shared with all who live there. The universe is orderly and organized according to divine law and intelligently administered by God's children.

God has created myriads of intelligent, living beings to perform many special functions. There are those very near to Divinity in perfection who have specific roles in God's plan, and then there are those perfecting beings, such as humans, who live on evolutionary worlds and are designed to reach perfection through experience. This is the "job" of humans. But like a kind and loving human parent, God wants His children to share the universe of His making. Just as the human parent desires to bring children into this world to experience life, so does God create a host of beings whom He loves and whom He hopes will learn to love Him in return. In actuality, God gives humans the gift of parenthood to share with Spirit the understanding of what parental love is, to begin to understand how God feels about us. As you love your own children, so does God love — but infinitely, eternally, and perfectly.

> Envisioning yourself communicating with God in a personal relationship cultivates the opportunity for you to know God as a loving person.

God's Plan for You

As the maker of the universe, God has a special plan for every created being. Viewing reality from the perspective of this planet, you may feel quite small, insignificant, and limited against the vast cosmos of the starry skies. It is difficult to view reality from such a narrow perspective: the larger picture of the universe is distorted or obscured. God's plan is vast and far-reaching, but you who live on this small world do not have this vantage point; therefore, your picture of reality is only the tiniest glimpse of an infinite canvas where the Artist is forever creating and perfecting creation's masterpiece. You may be quite unaware of what Spirit's plan is, yet it does exist. It is very real and it is unfolding right before your eyes. If you were to see reality with the eyes of the spirit, all the more clearly would you understand the nature of God's plan and where you as individuals fit in.

Thinking about the astonishing plan of the Universal Father/Mother for creation stimulates the imagination of His children to wonder about just what role in the unfolding universe each person will play. However, the surest and most fundamental way to discern that role is to recognize God as your spiritual parent and the importance of sharing within that relationship. For it is in the development of this relationship that you will come to recognize, feel, and understand the immense personal love God has for you and the joy-filled way our Creator wishes you to experience life in the universe. In developing a relationship with God, you will come to know your true self and how to best express your creative personality potential.

God, in the capacity of Divine Parent, has an infinite personality that is capable of having a relationship with each child. In knowing who God is, you will begin to understand Spirit's nature. God, as Spirit, is nothing less than the most loving, compassionate, kind, fair, understanding, forgiving, merciful friend and parent you will ever know. God is Spirit. And spiritual reality is everything that is true, beautiful, and good. So there is nothing in God's nature of hatred, anger, or jealousy. At the level of reality where Spirit resides, nothing exists that humans might consider ugly; it is nonexistent or unreal to God. There is nothing negative in the Universal Father/Mother; in Spirit there is only perfect goodness and love. However, at the level of reality where humans live, this is not so.

The potential for making mistakes exists on your planet because the world was not created in perfection; it is slowly evolving. You, as evolutionary beings, must learn from experience in order to evolve toward perfection. You have been given the gift of free will to choose what kind of life you will live and whether or not you will take the road to perfection. By your choice to behave in an error-prone manner – indulging in hatred, anger, envy, intolerance – you cut yourself off from God. You cannot feel Spirit's love for you when you are caught up in negative emotions. These are not of Spirit. They are unreal and, therefore, nonexistent to God. However, it is not that your Spiritual Parent has abandoned you. It is you that have cut yourself off from your Creator. Therefore, you must become reconnected. This occurs by developing an ongoing personal intimate relationship with God to keep your connection to Spirit strong and remain in Spirit's loving embrace.

> In developing a relationship with God,
> you will come to know your true self and
> how to best express your creative
> personality potential.

How God Feels about You

The best illustration depicting how God feels about you can be drawn from your experiences in loving relationships. A most helpful example is the parent-child relationship. While no one has had perfect parents, and may even have been abused by their parents, you can still imagine what an ideal parent would be like. Look to God as the ideal parent, for in reality your Divine Creator is just that. God is the one who loves you unconditionally and intimately, the one who understands your motivations, the one who knows your shortcomings, the one who is always by your side. As responsible and good human parents look at their child with love and understanding, so does the Universal Father/Mother view each one of His precious children.

But how much greater is our Father/Mother's love, compassion, mercy, forgiveness, understanding, and tenderness! God knows each child in detail and tenderly loves everyone in spite of their shortcomings. There is nothing our Spiritual Parent does not understand. There is no mistake, no sin, God cannot forgive, for Spirit knows all motivations. Our Creator knows you better than you know yourself. Realize there is nothing you can do to turn God away from you! It is you who turn away from God.

Why do you turn away? You may live in fear due to your concept of God. You may hide because you think Deity is angry with you or is punishing you for your misdeeds by inflicting disease or misfortune. Perhaps you find it difficult to believe in God because you do not understand why so much evil exists on this world. How unfortunate it is to think of God as wanting to punish you for your mistakes. How sad it is to blame God for humanity's errors! This attitude is inconsistent with the concept of an all-loving, all-forgiving, compassionate and merciful parent. These ideas are the greatest impediments in having a loving relationship with our wonderful Father/Mother.

How you hurt yourself when you turn away! God only wants to comfort you. Our Father/Mother is waiting to give you solace, understanding and, most of all, compassionate love as the balm to heal your wounds. You will feel the great personal love God feels for you if you ask for Spirit's help. This perfect love is there for the asking! The Universal Father/Mother, as creator of the universe, has infinite love, wisdom, and goodness to bestow at any time. These spiritual gifts are freely shared with you if you are willing to turn to God and ask.

You may not recognize that our good Father/Mother is personally with you every moment of every day of your life. Spirit's watchcare overshadows your life, but you are unaware. Like the child who insists on learning things on his or her own, so do you experience reality without the benefit of one who has greater knowledge. Who among you, as a parent, does not know you have more experience and wisdom than your child and wish your child would consult you when he or she is confused? How much greater is God's wisdom, how much greater is Divine understanding and compassion.

How much greater is God's love! Why do you not partake of this greater wisdom? Our Parent is so wise, so compassionate, so understanding. God knows what is best for you because Spirit is your source of life.

Human beings are dependent upon the Divine Father/Mother, this source, for all true sustenance of a spiritual nature. This is especially significant in light of people's attempts to understand the best way to live. Again, return to the idea of God as being a loving, compassionate, and merciful parent to understand how God relates to you in helping you achieve spiritual independence. When young children act foolishly or unthinkingly, they must experience the consequences of their actions. However, if they were to ask and follow the advice of the loving and wise parent as to the best approach to a situation, then would they learn the better way to handle life's circumstances. The parents have experience and wisdom to impart to their child. Likewise, your Father/Mother knows the better way and wishes to guide you. God desires only what is best for you.

> Our Father/Mother is waiting to give you solace, understanding and, most of all, compassionate love as the balm to heal your wounds. You will feel the great personal love God feels for you if you ask for Spirit's help. This perfect love is there for the asking!

2

The Human Approach to God

Seeing Yourself with the Eyes of God

It may be insightful in light of your developing relationship with God to view yourself as a small child. You are born as a tiny babe, helpless to all your surroundings, yet born with this enormous capacity to receive love. This is built into your physical mechanism. The budding personality develops and grows strong when it is nurtured by the character-building waters of unconditional love.

While you are created to live in physical material reality, there is another dimension that exists as your destiny: the spiritual realm. Your capacity for receiving love is what propels you toward this other dimension. You have been created to experience eternal life; therefore, our Creator sees you as an eternity child, one who requires many years of experience, spanning eons of time, before your potential is realized.

This first life on the physical world is your beginning. Even though you may spend sixty, seventy, or eighty years or more here, this is childhood of your eternal life – the first phase of your existence. Therefore, God views you much as you would view an infant or a small child of two, three, or four. How could you not love these precious little ones? They are so loving, so open, so trusting. This is how our Universal Father/Mother sees you, even when you act most negatively. His love for you never wavers, for Spirit understands you and knows that your potential will be achieved one day.

By seeing yourself as God views you, you will more fully understand our Spiritual Parent's loving nature. Then will you begin to trust Spirit's love and unlock your heart to feel this love, returning it to God. Love is the actual bond that our Father/Mother has created to kindle the relationship with His children. A very deep, nurturing love is what our Creator feels for each child. God knows each individual intimately, and lavishly pours Spirit's love upon each person, regardless of who they may be in the scheme of creation. No one is greater than any other in God's eyes. All are loved equally, no matter what their ability, level of intelligence, or status in the world; no reason exists that would cause the Universal Father/Mother to love you less than another.

There are no special chosen people of God. In spite of humanity's attempts to understand Divinity through various religious traditions, doctrines, rituals, and dogmas, God's love for the individual transcends these man-made institutions. It is humanity's limited perspective that dictates that God's love is only for certain people. It is humanity's concepts of God that fall short of the true comprehension of Spirit's loving nature.

> No reason exists that would cause the Universal Father/Mother to love you less than another.

The Significance of God's Love

God creates love itself as the internal link through which we experience life. Spirit uses this love to bestow and express the beauty of God's feeling toward each child and toward the whole universe. If it were not for love, reality would be devoid of meaning, value, and purpose, for no meaningful relationships would exist. As God loves you, so you are to love others; this is the supreme rule of life that our Universal Father/Mother has established for the functioning of the universe. You who live on this planet must learn to love more in order to improve the quality of your life. You need to trust the love our Creator has given to you.

Loving God and sharing love with others with whom you come in contact are the greatest secrets to a happy life. Sharing spiritual love and spreading it to others until the entire planet is overcome by this glorious energy are the two greatest privileges and joys of human existence. Only then will this world overcome its struggle with evil and emerge from its miseries.

The best and most direct way to transform this world is for each and every individual to turn to our Father/Mother God, thereby allowing the Spirit of God to flow through us, for within the hearts of transformed individuals there is no room for hate, anger, greed, or jealousy. These are spiritual unrealities. They may be emotional realities, but they are mere shadows of a displaced hunger for a spiritual connection.

To personally experience the presence of unconditional love in daily living transforms your life into one where your actions are based upon the highest ideals and the values of everything that is true, beautiful, and good. You become happy, patient, kind, compassionate, tolerant, generous, and courageous. This is God's promise to you! You grow confident and secure in the gifts our Universal Father/Mother gives to those who ask to feel Spirit's love. Who would not want to feel that every day? Would you not desire the joy and peace that developing a relationship with God yields?

It is all within your reach. Inner joy and peace is achieved by going within and asking it to be given to you. Ask and you shall receive. Our wonderful Spiritual Parent is waiting to enfold you in loving arms.

Like children who punish themselves because they feel unworthy or because they don't believe, you may have allowed yourself to be cut off from God. But to become reconnected simply requires an act of faith, nothing more. You are a child of God. Recognize this fact and let yourself be loved.

> By seeing yourself as God views you, you will more fully understand our Spiritual Parent's loving nature. Then you will begin to trust Spirit's love and unlock your heart to feel this love, returning it to God.

Difficulties Humans Face in Approaching God

The ability to feel and know the love of God is lying dormant within your hearts, minds, and souls. But most people do not recognize that it is there. Most individuals have not been raised to develop a personal relationship with God, nor do they understand how to accomplish this. Spiritual development has usually been relegated to religious institutions, which generally focus on dogma and ritual, with little attention being paid to feeling the personal presence of your Creator in everyday living. How many times do you take a break during the day to commune with our Father/Mother? Yet, if you were to do this throughout the day, you would find yourself being uplifted and transported beyond the problems you experience. You would find a realm of tranquility and rest, and in this repose you would find the strength and other spiritual coping tools you need to accomplish the tasks you must perform or handle the problems you face.

Learning to surmount challenges in life is what allows you to transcend the wide gap between your animal nature and the spiritual component of your being. Since you are in part a product of evolution from animal ancestry, your behavior can be very primal at times. On the other hand, you were made in God's image by being given sensing abilities within your mind to recognize spiritual reality – all that is true, beautiful, and good. Your spiritual nature can be, at times, contradictory with your animal nature, particularly when you may not like making choices that could compromise how comfortable you feel. You evolve spiritually by overcoming those tendencies that compose the portion of your makeup that you share with animals. By your choices you move from animal self-centeredness to spiritual self-forgetfulness, which aligns and balances your sense of self with your valuing of others.

But spiritual living is not honed on a playing field of ease and complacency. Spirituality is sharpened by those decisions that are placed before you in the guise of opportunities and challenges. These opportunities underscore deeper meanings that are designed to challenge you to embrace the greater truths God has created for living in the universe and for universal functioning. God knows what these truths are, but you cannot see them. Spiritual growth, then, lies in the tension of your comfort-seeking animal nature being pitted against those divine ideals within your mind. Those ideals encourage you to bring forth those noble qualities of your character that elevate human life to more enlightened levels. How can civilization advance when its citizens stagnate in the lower, base tendencies of their animal nature?

Developing your spirituality – your relationship with God – accomplishes the goal of living these divine ideals. As you awaken to feel Spirit's love and allow it to flow into your being, you accept yourself as a child of our Divine Creator. Your capacity for self-love increases and you begin to want to share this love with others. Your sense of identity expands as you keenly realize that as God's child, you have a place in the universe; you become increasingly aware of your potential and your destiny. This yearning for self-expression stimulates the urge to continue growing as you come to recognize that our Father/Mother God has a purpose for you as well as for the universe.

Attainment of the highest understanding of spiritual values is the goal for individuals, as well as for the civilizations of the physical worlds. How much you wish to contribute to your world's destiny is proportional to the amount of spiritual growth you wish to achieve while you live here, thereby increasing your capacity for happiness and fulfillment.

Ultimately, faith and trust in God yield bountiful spiritual riches. Feeling love is the very best inducement to doing good, bringing you more liberty, happiness, peace, and joy of living than could otherwise be imagined. The shackles of fear and uncertainty are broken. You know who you are. There is peace of mind and contentment that flies in the face of despair.

All of this is within your grasp. Use your imagination to envision what your life might be like if you felt this love as your stimulus to live. You have the capacity to feel that powerful love motivating your actions. You could, potentially, experience it every day if you wish. Awaken to the happiness sleeping inside you. Awaken to the spirit of God within waiting to make contact with you.

How many times do you take a break during the day to commune with God? Yet, if you were to do this throughout the day, you would find yourself being uplifted and transported beyond the problems you experience.

3

God's Gift – The Inner Spirit

The Role of the Inner Spirit

You, the children living on the worlds of evolution, have within your mind a divine fragment of the Universal Father. God gives each of you an actual piece of Spirit's nature with its divinity attributes (Truth, Beauty, and Goodness) as the link between you and the Divine Being. God is geographically separated from you by the vast expanse of space He creates, yet this fragment of Spirit lives within you as our Creator's means of maintaining contact with His children who live so far away. Since you cannot see God, this piece of divinity is the gift of Spirit to assist the children of time and space in the discernment of spiritual reality. While you will never attain the totality of God, you can become perfectly attuned to our God's will and love through your interaction with your inner spirit fragment. It acts as the receptacle for the love God has for you, as the guide to assist you to discern that which is true, and helps you to truly appreciate and seek spiritual values.

Were it not for this spirit presence, your lives would be little more than animal in nature; it is actually what separates you from the animals. Your inner spirit presence elevates you to the future acquirement of spiritual status by virtue of its presence within your mind. You evolve toward perfection as the spirit fragment guides you toward God.

Your life on this planet is so largely material, and so much time and effort is vested in the tangible pursuits of maintaining your physical existence, that you may not see or understand there is another dimension of reality. Reality is composed of three types of matter and energy: material, mind, and spiritual. Your access to the level of spiritual reality lives within your mind as the inner spirit. This link to the greater reality of the spiritual dimension exists just beyond the five physical senses. The spirit fragment dwells in a portion of your mind called the superconscious and, for the most part, lies dormant because you may not recognize the spiritual component to your being. Whether you call it the higher self, inner pilot, inner advisor, inner light, spirit of God, Holy Spirit, or any other name, this spirit is waiting to make contact with you and to lead you into the beautiful world of spiritual reality. You could not be attuned to Spirit without this.

Because of God's great love for you, He wants you to benefit from the joys of spiritual living. The inner spirit makes the reality of love, truth, beauty and goodness alive within you, should you desire to open yourself to its leadings. This is the mechanism God uses to link Spirit to the children living so very far removed from the Creator's domicile at the center of the universe, Paradise. It actually accompanies you as you go through life. You experience no thought, word, or deed without the knowledge of God by way of your inner spirit fragment.

God, in infinite wisdom and love, gave you this indwelling spirit so you can become perfectly attuned to divine ideals and values, enabling you one day to see Spirit – to actually stand in God's presence. You will, through the fusing with your inner spirit, be able to reach a perfected state of existence through experience and evolution. God has directed you to become perfect as Spirit is perfect, and this cooperative union between human and spirit is the way to attain this status. The divine spirit within helps you ascend step by step until the day you stand before God at the heavenly center of creation.

Thus, the spirit fragment eventually returns its ward to its Divine Source. This is the goal of the children living on evolutionary worlds. It is God's plan for the children of evolutionary worlds to have the inner potential for eternal existence. Thereafter, your destiny is to live eternally, giving love and sharing it with others through devoted learning about and service to God's never-ending creation. It truly is a magnificent destiny!

> This is the greatest gift to humans – the Universal Father/Mother bestowing the spirit as the pilot, allowing you to recognize Spirit's will for your life. For in cooperating with the divine guide, you can finally attain eternal status, culminating in a face-to-face meeting with our Universal Parent Source.

How the Inner Spirit Works in Human Life

As a personal gift from our Universal Father and Mother, your inner spirit is tailored to you in accordance with your evolutionary genetic inheritance plus your capacity for intellectual comprehension and spiritual receptivity. Your spirit fragment volunteers to indwell you based upon your overall personality components. And while residing in your mind, it carries a life plan that is projected throughout the course of your lifetime, beginning with life on this world, and all the way to eternity. This is the ideal life plan. It has its basis in perfect wisdom and goodness since its source is God.

However, because you are given free will to make choices, you can accept or reject this plan once you are fully aware of the consequences of your choice. The spirit fragment is given to you and is with you always. It patiently awaits your decision to choose whether or not to follow its leadings.

The inner spirit has key responsibilities. The most important of these are: first, to make conscious within the mind of its indwelling subject the great personal love of God, and second, to teach certain spiritual lessons that the spirit (as the perfect source of inner wisdom) knows will lead the individual to a much greater understanding of the nature of universal reality and of the Universal Father/Mother. Your inner spirit desires a personal relationship with you just as a good friend might desire your companionship, or as parents desire a loving relationship with their child.

But beyond that, your spirit wants to give you the greater understanding of its Source. God, as the source of the personal inner spirits, has all the answers to every question you will ever ask, even for your most troubling problems. All you need to do to answer the questions of your life is to ask the inner spirit and then listen. If you sincerely do wish to discern the answers in a spiritual manner – in a way that gives greater understanding of God's ways, or the universal laws of truth – then the spirit guide will gladly and patiently assist you to learn that which you most wish to know.

The inner spirit often encounters difficulty in its attempt to help you to learn and benefit from the beauty of spiritual reality. One of the biggest stumbling blocks is the basic animal nature, which naturally looks for the easiest and fastest way to do things. However, the laws of animals do not apply to humans. The easiest and fastest way to do things is usually not the God-given way. Your inner spirit guides you to discern a better way to live – the way established by God. The way of Spirit is the correct path because you learn the elements and laws of universal reality that enhance your ability to handle living with courage, grace, poise, strength, wisdom, and goodness. But you alone must choose which path to take.

The path of living according to God's eternal laws – the perfect and spiritual way of living – is long and filled with lessons to master in order to glean the deep realities of spirit. Those who are really up for this eternity journey of attaining perfection will pace themselves with patience and courage, harmonizing growth with wisdom and insight. Choices are put in your path that pit ease against effort, complacency against challenge, doubt against faith. And all this is up to you to choose. Your free will commands your path.

> If you sincerely wish to discern the answers in a spiritual manner – in a way that will give you greater understanding of God's ways, or the universal laws of truth – then the spirit guide will gladly and patiently assist you to learn that which you most wish to know.

The Human Choice to Be Spirit-Led

Our Universal Father/Mother, in infinite love, has given you free will to choose whether or not to seek spiritual living. This is not to make life difficult for you, but is done for a very inspiring reason. God is your spiritual parent. Just as human parents desire their children to know and love them of their own choice, so does our Creator allow you this free-will choice to know and love Him, or to ignore or even reject this spiritual kinship. God will not force you to love and honor Him; you must desire this and actively seek it.

Free will may impede you from growing spiritually and from feeling God's love if there is no desire on your part to seek a reality other than at the material/physical level. Always must your spirit subjugate itself to your will. Although God has given you the ability to make the decisions about your life and what course of living you will pursue, and not even the inner spirit can coerce you to do anything you do not wish to do. Free will as such is a sacred gift of the Universal Father and Mother. Your inner spirit must always respect your ability to choose and accept the consequences of your choices, even when you choose to engulf yourself in harmful self-recrimination and self-abusing actions. When you choose to ignore the spiritual values of truth, beauty, and goodness, your life becomes entangled in a quagmire of limited thinking and error. And since this dynamic applies to the way most people live, the cumulative effects have culminated in the many evils existing on this world: greed, hatred, anger, and other diseases of the spirit.

As a consequence of ignoring the spiritual dimension, most people live their lives stumbling over the rocks of their own choosing. Error after error is made; lessons must be repeated often before the understanding that the inner spirit wishes to impart is even minimally gleaned. How long will you continue to falter when the answers to your questions and problems lie within you, yearning to be heard? How many lessons must be repeated until you awaken to the voice of the spirit guiding you to choose things in the correct or spiritual way, thus leading you to understanding and insight? Most people still seek answers from external sources – other people or society's experts – when the most loving, perfect, wise, fair, and compassionate friend you will ever have lives within your mind and is ready to impart all it knows to you

> Although God has given you the ability to make the decisions about your life and what course of living you will pursue, not even the inner spirit can coerce you to do anything you do not wish to do.

Human Cooperation
with the Inner Spirit

God's will for you is twofold: that you have a relationship with Spirit, and that you treat your fellow brothers and sisters – the children of God – with patience, forgiveness, compassion, tolerance, kindness, humility, honesty, and love. This is living according to God's ways. The goal of the spirit is to lead the human of its indwelling to a life based on yielding the fruits of the spirit. Thus, making contact with your inner spirit is the most important experience you can have while living the physical life on your planet. There is nothing more important, more necessary, or that will help you to live a fuller, healthier and happier life. If it is your desire to feel more love, if you desire happiness, seek the leadings of your spirit. If you want to overcome your personality shortcomings, if you desire more insight into your identity, seek the leadings of the spirit. If you want to improve the relationships within your family or with friends, seek the leadings of your spirit. Spiritual growth is the essence of living a happier life; it is the secret of living.

As with anything worthwhile or valuable, it takes time and dedication to grow in the spirit. You cannot say to yourself, "I want to grow spiritually," and think that you have become enlightened. Nor can you assume that it is sufficient to know our Creator intellectually without feeling God's love or expressing this love in your life. Spiritual growth comes from effort, it comes from insight, it comes from choosing to live dedicated to those higher ideals that ennoble the human experience. Spiritual living is active; it does not hide from the difficulties of life. Spiritual living means meeting life's challenges with faith and hope. Spiritual living truly means sharing your love with others.

To play the melodies and harmonies of beautiful music, a musician must master the craft. Spiritual growth may be compared to the desire to play a musical instrument; many years of practice and dedication are required before the music student becomes a master. You must desire spiritual growth, foremost, but then you must practice making contact daily with your spirit to allow the environment of your mind to become fertile for the inner spirit to plant its seeds. In truth, it is then and only then that your mind – your conscious thoughts – will bear fruits that steer the actions of your daily life in a positive direction. Then and only then will you find happiness, contentment, and peace beyond your wildest imaginings. With God as the conductor of your orchestral body, the melody of your life will resonate to the heavens!

The road to perfection is long and is filled with many twists and turns. Diversions on the path are sometimes encountered when an honest, searching soul tries to sort through the decisions of human living with a limited viewpoint based solely on a material perspective. How much easier it would be to stay on the road to happiness and joy were you to turn to the surest pilot resident within your mind. How much more quickly would you understand who you are and love yourself, how much more quickly would your life's lessons be learned if the Divine Pilot within your mind were used to master the skills you need to meet the challenges existing in life. Exchanging the ideas harbored in your mind for the information of your Divine guide is an effective way to accomplish this. Listening to the inner voice of Spirit speak to your mind is the beginning of the journey.

> Making contact with your inner spirit is the most important lesson you can learn while living the material life on your planet.

4

The Voice of the Inner Spirit

To exchange the Divine Mind in place of your own mind means to do God's will. By going within and listening to your inner voice, you will find the messages of Spirit's counsel becoming clearer and your love for God blooming. This internal relationship with our Eternal Father/Mother is the bedrock upon which character is built. It is the fortress that protects you as you face life's difficulties. It is the foundation for spiritual growth.

Human Mind Interference with the Inner Voice

The soil for spiritual growth is the mind. Crops of spiritual riches of peace, love, joy, and happiness can be harvested by listening to the inner voice of your spirit, but you may not immediately hear the answers. In order to communicate with you, your spirit must pierce through layers of conscious and unconscious thoughts. You have many pre-existing ideas and perceptions about certain issues that the spirit may find difficult to penetrate. Since you have free will, your inner spirit must circumnavigate the barriers arising from your thoughts and emotions, looking for openings in your perceptions and beliefs through which it can help you glimpse truth.

Your mind is constantly active; endless thoughts are entering and meandering through your consciousness. In addition to conscious level, there is the realm of unconscious thought, which houses your desires, fears, anxieties, and memories. These mental inputs flow in and out of your mind, causing you to wonder what it all means. Your decisions, and resulting actions, are based on these influences. Also, your inner life – your thoughts, ideals, and dreams – is constantly conditioned by external belief systems as well as bombarded by the evils of the culture: anger, hatred, greed, bigotry. These mental toxins can pollute your mind, seeping easily into your conscious and unconscious thoughts, slowly poisoning your decisions and actions. It is little wonder that your inner spirit encounters such difficulty in trying to communicate with you. It is little wonder both your inner and outer world is in such chaos.

Your divine spirit dwells at the highest level of your mind – in the superconscious level – a subtle level of which most humans are unaware. However, if you were to desire the guidance of your inner spirit instead of relying only on your own intellect and experience to help you meet the many challenges in your life, your inner spirit could reach down into the various levels of mind. The spirit could relay information to help you discern the better way and motivate you to follow the best path. Thus, the way to prepare the soil of your mind to receive this information is through "seeking the stillness." A stilled mind will allow the spirit to imprint its leadings onto your consciousness.

While you may not understand exactly how the mind works, you can clearly sense that there is a constant interplay between your waking thoughts and your deeper, only partly conscious, desires, longings, and fears. The highest longings are spiritual. These reside in your higher mind, the super-conscious. The human mind is the intermediary between the outside, material world and the inner spiritual reality. Your mind carries within it the answers to life's secrets – and the potential to understand the great cosmic mysteries in the realm of spirit. In order to tap in to this vast well of truth and knowledge, you must quiet your mind to partake of the deep spiritual currents running through it. Thus, your mind hovers on the brink of great enlightenment!

Know that where the spirit leads, there is truth. No greater truth is contained anywhere than within the spirit. No human has greater understanding than the spirit, nor does any institution built by humankind. But the human mind has difficulty accessing spiritual information because of the rapid course of internal chatter – your thoughts based upon your experiences. This natural static creates blocks in reception of truth. So the relationship between Creator and human child does not flourish because the human mind at times blocks the reception of truth. The biggest impediment is the kind of conscious thinking that does not include God as part of your daily activities. The exchange of thoughts from Spirit to human will become greatly clarified if you consciously participate by asking to be guided in the proper direction.

> If you desire the guidance of your inner spirit instead of relying only on your own intellect and experience to help you meet the challenges in your life, your inner spirit could reach down into the various levels of mind. The spirit could relay information to help you to discern the better way and motivate you to follow the best path.

How Humans Grow Spiritually

Developing an personal relationship with our Universal Father/Mother and feeling God's love are the best ways to grow in truth discernment; these comprise spiritual growth itself. As this relationship grows, your inner spirit motivates you to accept and receive increasing amounts of divine love and guidance. A gradual transformation slowly unfolds as your conscious thoughts and decisions are gently reshaped. All of the spiritual ideas and principles you need in order to live successfully are contained in this fragment spirit of God within your mind. Since accessing divine information is achieved by allowing the mind to become quiet and reflective, tapping in to your inner resources is in actuality the direct path to God. This is how you access your link to Spirit.

The road to attain perfection is long indeed, and it is one that is constantly filled with new challenges and opportunities for growth. You were not born perfect; you must constantly seek, learn, and experience until you have mastered living in a spiritual way (doing God's will). This is how you have been designed, and it is useless to fight your inherent nature. However, accepting the experiential nature of the journey will help you to understand the process involved in growing spiritually.

Spiritual growth takes time, just as anything of value requires patience to be fully appreciated and experienced. The components of learning a new craft or skill are similar to the dynamics of spiritual growth. If you were to try to sculpt a statue, could you build a masterpiece in only one day? No! You must dedicate yourself to crafting and refining. You must persevere even when you do not feel you are learning anything new or cannot see how you are progressing. Sometimes you will feel stalled; you may feel discouraged and wish to stop. But if you really do stop, will you become the master artisan you desire to be? Spiritual growth is just like any other learning and mastering experience: You must practice over and over that which you value in order to master it. Over time you will progress in mastery.

As an experiential being, you were created to learn in this way, regardless of what field of endeavor you are engaged in. Your mind is structured to learn progressively, moving from one level of understanding to another. You reach one level of proficiency, where you immerse yourself in all you need to experience at that level, and then you proceed to the next level which, in turn, you must master. Your mastery of the lessons is based on the decisions you make that lead you to either glimpse new insights or to stay static in your current state. Your experiences teach you new concepts or ways to handle situations. Failure to grasp the meaning underlying the experience leads to repetition until insight and wisdom are attained.

The dynamic for spiritual growth is no different. The path of spiritual enlightenment requires you to encounter those situations that compel you to produce fruits that prove you have learned the lessons. You augment your enlightenment by cultivating those spiritual habits that produce the skills you need to perfect your craft and master your lessons. The lessons are structured so you will overcome those subtle patterns of behavior that do not reflect what is true, beautiful, and good – Godliness.

> Spiritual growth takes time,
> just as anything of value requires
> patience to be fully appreciated
> and experienced.

Overcoming Spiritual Blocks

You may be totally unaware you have blocks that hinder insight into your daily behavior. Fear, unworthiness, shame, despair, anger, guilt, rejection, intolerance, narrow-mindedness, and hate are poisons that impede your spirit from communicating with you. These great barriers are difficult to eradicate from your thinking and emotional expression. By their very nature, they block the flow of spiritual energy and information to your mind. They are in direct opposition to spiritual values and divine ideals – truth, beauty, goodness, love. These spirit poisons are very powerful inducements to negative behavior, and when left unchecked, fester into wounds that cannot be eliminated by mere acts of will, because they have immense power over you. You allow yourself to be controlled by negative emotions especially when you do not eliminate them positively.

Spiritual communion with God is the ideal remedy for these poisons, for there is no greater power or antidote than the positive nature of God's love. There is no evil that can withstand this force. Our Infinite Father/Mother's love is a superhuman power. It is the best solution to overcome these toxins. If you feel you are out of control with these negative emotions, if you feel you want to eliminate them from your thinking but are powerless to do so, then you need a superhuman power to help you. There is only one antidote. Allow God to take these poisons, your negative emotions, from you. Ask Spirit to help you overcome them. Ask God to replace anger with compassion. Ask to replace fear with courage. Ask to replace despair with hope. Ask for whatever you think would be the spiritual counterpart to your troubles. Call the problem or negative feeling up into your mind and ask our Father/Mother to transform its power over you. Ask Spirit to help you see what the spiritual antidote is.

There will always be a useful spiritual answer to your problems. Attuning yourself to the inner voice is the means to seek a spiritual answer to a material life problem or challenge. While you always have the choice whether or not to stay in a difficult situation, the assistance and guidance you need is at the spiritual level. Circumstances may not automatically change, but you will be given the spiritual tools of insight, wisdom, patience, forbearance, courage, hope, trust, love, and forgiveness to strengthen you as you work through the problem. God is mainly concerned about your spiritual well-being, about the way in which you react to life, your true attitude. The material circumstances of your life, for the most part, are reflective of your choices. How you react to these circumstances is the measure of your true spirituality – how well you transcend material challenges with the divine values of love, trust, faith, courage, and goodness.

On your path to spiritual enlightenment, God will never require you to be in a situation in which your physical safety, emotional well-being, and spiritual health are compromised. However, you may find yourself in difficult situations because of your life choices, society's conditions, or merely the fact that life on this world is imperfect. You must ask yourself in these challenging situations, "What do I need to help me out of this problem?" This is the opportunity to still your mind and directly ask your inner spirit what spiritual coping tools will support you through the challenge so you can triumph over the problem. If you are receptive, doing this will change your perspective and help you find your way out of the situation. It actually changes your outlook from a negative to a positive one. A positive attitude is the exchange of the very limited human viewpoint for the far-sighted divine perspective. It is an adjustment in your thinking. *Think of your inner spirit as a thought adjuster; it gradually and gently reshapes your thoughts to those reflective of spiritual reality.* Reacting to a difficult life situation with hope, courage, fortitude, perseverance, or forgiveness is the positive response fortified by true spiritual tools.

God wants to help you overcome your problems. Our Creator waits patiently for you to come to Spirit in order to do this, but you must seek His help. First you must choose to rid yourself of emotional toxins and negative thinking. Once you made the choice, then your spirit has the opportunity to communicate God's answers to you. When you turn your problems over to God, you allow Spirit's superhuman power of love and guidance to instill in your mind the greater insight you need. This is the giant leap forward in your spiritual development. God loves you and desires your happiness. Realize that you create many obstacles in your own quest for fulfillment by your reluctance to seek our Universal Father/Mother's perspective and help in understanding the lessons you must master as part of your ongoing character and spiritual development. The degree to which you trust God to show you a better way is the degree to which you are literally willing to eliminate your personal problems in a spiritual manner.

If you feel you are out of control with these negative emotions, if you feel you want to eliminate these from your thinking but are powerless to do so, then you need a superhuman power to help you. There is only one anti-dote. Allow God to take these poisons, your negative emotions, from you. Ask Spirit to help you overcome them.

Hearing the Inner Voice

Removing the many inner barriers that block your spirit's communication is the first step to hearing the inner voice of the spirit. Trust is a very important component of hearing the inner voice. Trust in God's love and desire for you to find fulfillment. Just as a friend cares for you and your welfare, you are always in our Creator's watchcare. As you spend time seeking the stillness relaxing in the state of spiritual communion and bask in the bright glow of the Universal Father/Mother's love, you develop the vital trust connection. Your sense of security in God's love grows stronger, and your trust in Spirit's guidance becomes more pronounced. Your ability to relinquish your fears and doubts to God – coupled with your increasing capacity to feel our Divine Creator's love in spiritual communion – sets the stage to receive your indwelling spirit's leadings.

This develops a state of mind that produces the restful, receptive flow of love and enlightenment. It allows the "static" in your direct line of communication with Spirit to gradually lessen so you can hear the signal from God better. However, at first you may not hear an answer. You must be patient. Allow time for your spirit's voice to penetrate your conscious mind. It may take a few minutes, a few days or weeks; it could take longer. Your receptivity is conditioned by your willingness to see things from God's viewpoint. And it depends on your willingness to be led by your indwelling guide, and to remove the barriers to communication, as well as your openness to receiving God's love. Your inner spirit knows exactly when you are ready to accept insight and guidance. You may think you are ready for the answers, but only your spirit knows when you are truly ready to accept the answer God wants you to know, the answer geared to your best interest. Therefore, it is very important to trust your Spiritual Parent to unveil to you in His own time the highest understanding you can accept.

The spirit voice is subtle. It works within your mind to gently guide you to new insights and understandings of spiritual reality – so you can appreciate reality from God's perspective. It takes time to discern and evaluate what these nuances of spirit guidance are trying to reveal. Your spirit is attempting to relay the meanings of spiritual values behind the lessons you need to learn, ones aimed at developing your character and personality potential.

However, the gentle impressions your spirit wishes you to hear may turn into a louder voice, especially if you are bent on following a path of your own choosing, that could lead to great harm or even destruction. You may find yourself in a crisis situation brought about by your stubborn reluctance to awaken your spiritual potential. It may be a life-threatening situation or one in which you feel great despair, causing you to cry out for a higher power to help you. In these cases, you may glimpse a flash of insight or the realization that help is available. This insight may create an immediate recogntion within to ask God to guide you through your crisis.

For some humans, receptivity is heightened during crises when your need is greatest or your current life situation is harmful. It is at these moments that your indwelling spirit can more easily convey the love and presence of God to you. Spirit gives you the strength you need to pull you through your despair. During these life-altering moments, you are more open to embrace greater truth and insights about the spiritual road to happiness and fulfillment; the better way to live comes more clearly into focus. Often, crisis produces the greatest spiritual growth.

Regardless of how the stage is set for your receptivity to the answers and insights to guide your life, however, the spirit speaks to you in many ways. You do not need to experience crisis to grow spiritually. Attuning yourself daily to God's guidance will gently and skillfully lead you to new understandings and insights about your life and the circumstances you encounter. Insight paves the way for your reasoning abilities and inner sensing mechanisms to adjust more closely with the spiritual values of goodness and truth. This is the harmonization of your ego with your spirit – the basic desires of your animal nature yielding to the higher ideals of the divine. This produces a gradual change in your perceptions about life, and this, over time, will change your actions. You can gauge how much you have grown by seeing how you react in difficult situations. If you can react positively when you may have formerly responded with a negative response, this indicates you have grown.

You can avoid crises altogether by offering your indwelling spirit the soil of your mind to plant the seeds of recognition, deep insight, and wisdom for better judgment, reasoning, and emotional self-control. Such an approach will improve your skills at handling whatever comes your way in a more spiritual fashion – with goodness. You will also notice that your temperament becomes more balanced; there will be fewer instances when you become angry or fearful. This reduces the stress and tension that so greatly inhibit happiness and health. The key lies in your ability to know where to look for your answers and what will sustain your strength. Going within should always be the first step. However, be aware that God also speaks through the lives of many people and through other external means, such as inspirational stories or seemingly coincidental occurrences. The genuine challenge is to recognize Spirit's voice whenever it communicates with you.

> Your receptivity is conditioned by your willingness to hear things from God's viewpoint.

Discerning the Voice of Spirit from the Human Mind

The challenge, of course is in interpreting your answers. No two people are alike. What feels right to you may not seem so to another. An idea that rings true to you may not be acceptable to another. Therefore, exercise great discretion in discerning your answers. God works in many ways. Your inner spirit is your subtle and gentle guide whose impressions upon your mind will come into the conscious forefront when you are ready to accept the answer. These may come from a book, or an idea may appear across your mind, or you may hear a word or a phrase. You may experience a dream that seems meaningful, or you may encounter a person whose words are inspiring or who offers you a new look at a concept or situation. These are the many ways the subtle voice of God speaks to you. Be flexible and open to accepting help in whatever form it may appear. Truth comes in many packages – it is as diverse as the personalities God creates to express His love. Everyone has gifts to express truth. Be available to all expressions of love and truth. You never know where your next answer will appear. You never know when you will encounter someone who could help you see reality in a broader and more insightful manner.

When you are given what seems to be an answer or when you are confronted with choices, especially difficult ones, ask yourself, "Will this decision bring me closer to God? Will this help me love myself and my brothers and sisters more? Will this answer assist me to better understand who I am? Will this choice produce feelings of love, of peace, of connection with God?"

In stillness communion with your spirit, directly ask for confirmation or clarification. In specific communication of this type, you begin to develop the **intuition** that helps you understand when it is the voice of your inner spirit leading you in a certain direction or when it is just your ego speaking. Over time, you deepen the trust bond, strengthening your ability to sense the true answer, either through a feeling or an insight. The feeling and/or insight will produce a sensing of rightness. Also ask yourself, "Will this decision bring God closer to me? Will the fruits of the spirit – love, kindness, patience, understanding, tolerance, compassion, strength, courage, and selflessness be manifested in my decision and actions?" These are guideposts that indicate whether or not you are acting in a God-like manner. These are spiritual values that our Universal Father/Mother has created to order reality. Use these as your guidelines to ascertain whether the answers to your choices are correct.

Except for times of crisis, usually your God-given fragment works in your life silently and patiently, waiting for the hour when you will seek and acknowledge the inner guide, who is lovingly urging you to embrace the spiritual path. You may be totally unaware how to access this spirit due to the lack of training from a very young age to cultivate habits that will foster listening to the inner voice, and those cultural influences that do not value spiritual growth as worthwhile.

Most people live without ever availing themselves of this wonderful helper, and thus lead very unfulfilling, even desperate lives. Most people do not recognize that they themselves and others have the spiritual potential to hear the voice of God and the capacity to receive God's love. You go about life alone and lost, paralyzed by its challenges, crippled by its unfairness, feeling betrayed by the cruelty of others, and blinded by the limitations of your thoughts. You cannot see your way out of the traps of material living or by the ones you have created for yourselves. You cannot see that there is help to overcome your difficulties or recognize how to attain a spiritually abundant life replete with the joys life has to offer. So much potential is lying dormant. So much love and happiness is sleeping, waiting for the hour when you ask your inner spiritual guide to ring the bell to awaken you to hear the truth.

Attuning to the voice of your indwelling God-given guide will change your perceptions, it will alter how you think about life and help you address your material problems and challenges with spiritual tools. In the stillness state of consciousness, you are exchanging your mind for the mind of our Creator. You are using your intuitive gifts to discern the higher values and principles of spiritual reality: goodness, truth and beauty — God-consciousness.

If you use only your logic, reason, and life experience to discern the answers to life's questions, you will fall short of the satisfaction you seek. Logic and reason are exercises of the intellect and do not reach the spiritual level of knowing our Divine Creator. The realm of the intellect is the human level of understanding, but the realm of the spirit is where truth reigns supreme. When you exchange your mind and ask to see things from God's viewpoint, then your inner spirit can tell you when something is true; Spirit can convey a signal that feels right. This is the inner way of knowing – both intuition and insight.

These keen, illuminating perceptions are gifts from our Divine Creator that will help you recognize the universal truths which guide you to the best way to live – to become more God-like. When you seek God only at the intellectual level, you will not find Spirit. You will not find happiness and joy, you will not experience peace and contentment. For God is the source, embodiment, and personification of these treasures which only exist at the spiritual level and flow directly from Him. Seek the stillness of Spirit, be with God, and everything true, good, and beautiful will come to you.

"Will this decision bring God closer to me? Will the fruits of the spirit – love, kindness, patience, understanding, tolerance, compassion, strength, courage, and selflessness be manifested in my decision and actions?" These are the guideposts indicating whether or not you are acting in a God-like manner.

5

Seeking the Stillness

"Be still and know that I am God." The essence of spiritual growth is this simple statement. Being still allows the inner spirit fragment the opportunity to send its messages to your mind. This, in turn, will make you conscious of the spirit's leadings, converting subtle inspiration into a way of life. Living, then, becomes a personal religion motivating you not only to do good, but also to seek continued enlightenment, to strive to know God and become Godlike.

Why Stillness Is Important

Communion with God, communion at the spiritual level, is the highest form of human communication. Talking with God transcends the state of mental relaxation because it gives the indwelling spirit the opportunity to imprint truth onto your mind. *When you have achieved a mental relaxation and stay at that level without reaching beyond to the spiritual level of communion with God, you will feel peaceful and perhaps blissful, but you will not reach the deeper level of enlightenment, understanding, and love that truly teaches you the best way to live.* Your inner spirit waits for this opportunity so that it can communicate our Creator's love to you.

It is in this state of spiritual communion that you will reap the greatest benefit. The love that our Universal Father/Mother pours over you is endless and unconditional; it stops only when you choose to break the connection. Being in this state of spiritual communication is the greatest motivator for building your spirituality. God's wish for you is to develop this state of being so you can truly feel that Spirit loves you and is with you always. Can you think of a more healing power than this? God's love heals all: It banishes anger, self-doubt, and fear by the intense power of goodness.

The longer you can stay in the flow of our Creator's love, the more insight and understanding you gain to help you structue your life in a more productive and positive way. Your life will improve as you are given the tools you need to rid yourself of the excess baggage of fear. You feel uplifted, you feel transported to the realm where love is the only law, where you get a taste of living as a spiritual being in God's family. The more love you feel, the greater your capacity to grow spiritually, to seek enlightenment, and to attain the happiness you desire. The only real stumbling block to a truly satisfying life is an unwillingness or lack of desire to share your inner life with Spirit.

The human tendency is to not seek communion with the inner spirit of God. This is because you have not been trained in childhood to still your mind or encouraged to develop a personal relationship with God. How, then, can you reasonably expect to be able to discern just what Spirit is trying to say to you when the mindal ground for spiritual seeds to be planted has not been properly cultivated? The treasures of listening to your inner voice are greater peace, greater self-awareness, and self-love and love for others, but it does not happen overnight, especially when ingrained habits accumulated over your lifetime overtake your best intentions to follow your spirit's leadings. Be very patient and nonjudgmental with yourself; allow yourself some time to familiarize yourself with this process of attuning to the inner voice. But a regular, well-ordered practice can help you begin and support you as you grow more comfortable in sharing your life with God.

God's love heals all: it banishes anger, self-doubt, and fear by its intense power of goodness. The longer you can stay in the flow of our Creator's love, the more insight and understanding you gain to help you structure your life in a more productive and positive way.

The Stillness Practice

There is no magic formula for reaching the state of stillness, but there are general guidelines to make it more successful.

The most important objective in practicing stillness is consistency. You will benefit the most if you practice daily. Practicing the stillness every single day will form a habit, a spiritual habit, which then becomes a key part of your daily routine. It is not required to do it at the same time every day; but it is helpful to do so while you are getting started.

Choose a time when you can truly escape from the pressures of family and work life. Even though life is very busy and it may almost seem impossible to incorporate stillness into your day, envision this time as your retreat into the realm of peace and beauty – a mental vacation. Try to set aside twenty to thirty minutes when you will not be interrupted. If this is too much time, then just do what you can, even if it is for five minutes. But do try to practice it every day for as long a time as you can. You can do this in your home or outdoors, whatever is your preference. Remember, you are trying to develop a daily habit that will, over time, lead you to doing it automatically. You will find that you look forward to this time of quiet reflective communion; you will need it almost as much as the air you breathe.

The Seven Steps of Stillness

1. Get Physically Relaxed

The first step is to become completely physically relaxed. You want to create a state of total relaxation and peace. Your goal is to eliminate all tension and stress from your body. A popular position you may want to consider using is to sit upright in a comfortable chair with your feet on the ground. You may also lie down, but you might fall asleep, especially at first, since this is the initial response of your mind when you begin to unwind. Since you want to spend this time with God, it is better to stay relaxed but alert. Choose a position that is comfortable and will keep you awake. It also is quite helpful to pick a time of day when you will be alert. Practicing before bedtime may put you to sleep, so daytime stillness is more productive.

Now, take in several deep breaths and allow all the tension to leave your body. Imagine that with each inhalation you are allowing God's love to enter your body, and with every exhalation, tension and worries depart. Repeat this breathing until you feel a sense of relaxation. You may feel energy enter at your feet. Envision this gentle power running up your legs, your torso, into your arms, and up, out the top of your head.

These may be feelings you experience for the first time during physical relaxation. Do not be alarmed if you feel a tingling sensation or a warm rush of energy. You are allowing your body to receive the energy that is naturally occurring in the universe. This energy has a tremendous healing effect since its source is God. Think of it as a loving, beneficent force regenerating your body. Even if you are unable to achieve the next levels of stillness about to be discussed, you will find that just this deep relaxation leaves you more refreshed and give you greater stamina when you practice it regularly. However, if you do wish to continue your stillness at the point when you feel very relaxed, you are ready to begin to still your mind.

2. Get Mentally Relaxed

While the phrase "stilling the mind" implies that your mind stops thinking and becomes totally empty, what you are trying to do is actually to rid your mind of all the endless chatter that fills it. Ideas such as, "What will I eat for dinner" or "What will I wear tomorrow" or "The kids are driving me crazy" still linger from the day, but right now is the time to distance yourself from them. You are trying to quiet your mind in order to concentrate on communicating with God. The true goal of stillness is to focus your thoughts on God exclusively.

To help your mind rid itself of the internal commotion, it might be helpful to listen to uplifting instrumental music for all or part of the time. Vocal music may distract you, so try to use only instrumental pieces, especially those which elicit feelings of joy and tranquility. Also, you might find that picturing yourself in a beautiful environment is most conducive to relaxing your mind. Or you may picture yourself with someone you love – visual imagery is an effective means to still the mind. But this is a personal choice. There is no one right way. The best way for you is whatever you find evokes this state the most easily and helps you stay relaxed. The key element in achieving mental stillness is being able to stay centered on the one thing (your focal point) that is evoking peaceful, loving feelings. Centering your thoughts on this will bring about feelings of happiness, serenity, and a deep sense of well-being.

If your mind wanders – and it will many times – simply refocus on whatever it is you are using to relax – the music or the visual imagery, for example. You will have to do this quite frequently, but do not be discouraged. Above all, do not reproach or judge yourself for not being able to be still for long periods of time. When you first start doing stillness, you find that your mind wants to stay fairly active. This is normal. Preventing your mind from wandering is the most difficult part of all. Even if you only achieve mental stillness for a few seconds, it is the beginning. Over time you will find that you can stretch these moments of stillness into a few minutes or even longer. This is why daily practice and repetition is so important. You will get better with continued practice. You will find it easier to still your mind and stay focused on what you wish to achieve in your communication with God.

Stay in this state of mental relaxation for as long as you wish. Enjoy the currents of energy flowing through you. Linger in your feelings of warmth, calmness, and comfort.

Be good to yourself. You deserve this relaxation time. You work hard, you have a busy life. Take this time out and envelop yourself in tranquility and beauty. This is your bastion in the midst of life's conflicts.

You may find yourself wandering from your point of focus; you may see images and colors flash across your mind. Do not be concerned — this is the natural movement of your mind. Just gently bring it back to your point of concentration, your focal point, and bask in the loving warmth surrounding you. Stay there and rest until you feel compelled to begin your conversation with God. You will sense when you are ready to do this.

3. Talk to God

Communion with God is your goal in seeking the stillness. Once you have centered yourself in mental relaxation and feel the music or imagery deep within, you will feel a warm sense of connection, of wholeness. This is your signal that you are ready to start talking to God. Next, imagine yourself being in Spirit's presence. By envisioning God through whatever conceptual pictures you prefer, you foster a sense of personal communication. You could envision God as a beautiful force or light surrounding you; it could be an image of a person holding your hand; it may be a mother loving you; it could be imagining yourself as a child lying in loving arms. Whatever you envision God to be is very personal to you and is the right picture. No one visualization is correct. Each person will view God uniquely. But your goal is to see yourself in a relationship with God, actually to feel God with you.

When you have envisioned God in whatever form

you desire, begin to talk to your Creator to your heart's content. God wants your doubts, fears, problems, desires, and joys. Say whatever you wish to say. Share your feelings and thoughts. God is intimately acquainted with all of your thoughts and feelings; there is no secret, guilt, or shame unrevealed to Spirit. However, from the human standpoint, talking to God affords you the opportunity to recognize where you need help and creates a receptivity to being guided by your Divine Parent. So, freely share all aspects of your life with God – positive and negative.

4. Ask for Help

As you tell God about your problems, ask for help to work through them. Request from God the spiritual antidotes of patience, forgiveness, understanding, and also compassion, instead of anger, hate, fear, and other negative emotions. Talk with God as if you were with the most loving parent or person imaginable, for in reality you are. Ask to be filled with Spirit's love. Ask for Divine Parental guidance. Ask about anything that perplexes or troubles you. You will never find a more sympathetic listener or compassionate friend.

You are a beloved child of the God, and your Divine Mother/Father wants to love and support you through life. It is important to ask for help, however, because you have free will. God does not offer advice or guidance without your permission. Identify what it is you need from Spirit so it can be offered to you. If you are not sure of what to ask, simply say to God, "What do I need to do right now in order to grow spiritually?"

5. Give Thanks

In the act of requesting help from God, a sense of support and connection is conveyed to your mind. In turn, this feeling yields a sense of thankfulness. You can continue, then, by offering your appreciation for all of life's goodness and blessings. Thank Spirit for the good things in your life, because Spirit is the source. Offer praise for the beauty, magnitude, and glory of our Eternal Father/Mother's being.

Thanksgiving is a natural phase of spiritual communion that deepens the child/Spiritual Parent bond. You appreciate what God has given you, and in turn, your receptivity to feeling God's love increases. This is the springboard for building your relationship. You recognize what God does for you because of Spirit's great love for you. You open the way for communication from God to begin, allowing the current of love to flow between you and God.

6. Listen to God

Once you have spent time talking with God, asking for help, and giving thanks, the other half of the communication process is to listen. Listening to what God has to say is the foundation for your thoughts and behaviors to become more spirit-led and God-like.

By talking with God and offering trust at the human end, you give your spirit the permission it needs to communicate truth and shower love upon you. Cooperating with your inner spirit is fundamental to your continued growth since your free will cannot be superseded. You cannot benefit from the wisdom of the spirit's leadings and feel God's love unless you truly desire it. Growing spiritually is a choice. The desire to be with God needs to come from you. No one will ever try to force you, not even our Universal Father/Mother.

But if you choose to develop this relationship, then it will be worthwhile only if you listen to what Spirit wants to say to you. Communication is a two-way street. In this sense, God is no different from someone else who wishes to talk to you. You would enter willingly into communication if you wanted to be in a relationship with another person. You can also do this with your Spiritual Parent.

So at this stage of your stillness, listen for God's answer by allowing your mind to be still for as long as you are able, just as if this wise counselor were sitting by your side speaking to you. When you converse with someone, you allow your mind some time of repose as you listen to what the other person is trying to convey. The signal conveyed by your spirit will reach your mind more efficiently when you listen inwardly. You cultivate an increasingly receptive environment when your focus is attuned to listening to your inner voice. It takes time, dedication, and perseverance to attune yourself to this inner leading; however, if you practice consistently, you will be indeed richly rewarded.

At this stage, when you are seeking insight or answers to your questions, allow your mind to be totally open to listening. Your inner spirit will begin to communicate with you. Tune your listening inside. Wait as long as you can and maintain your listening focus. Depending upon your receptivity and your ability to remove the barriers to communication, colors, pictures, words, or ideas may flash across your mind. Do not try to interpret any of these. Simply continue to listen. This is your spirit's opportunity to communicate to you. The longer you can focus on this inner listening, the longer will your indwelling spirit have to impart to your conscious mind what it feels you are ready to receive.

7. Sense the Divine Presence

Our loving Divine Father/Mother stands ready to lavish you with unimaginable love and beauty. Envision Spirit showering you with divine affection, as if you were standing under a shower of loving rain. Actually ask God to send the Divine presence and love flow through you, and offer your love back. This is the culmination of the personal relationship with God. In this state of stillness, you are getting to know the Universal Father/Mother. You are sensing and learning about God's loving, merciful nature. You are in touch with Spirit's infinite compassion, are receiving tender mercy, and bountiful understanding. In opening yourself and asking for guidance for your life, you are learning to accept that God loves you.

The dynamic of coming to know God is similar to learning to know another person. Just as you need to communicate and spend time with someone in order to truly know who he or she is, so you need to communicate with God in order to benefit from Spirit's goodness. However, in human relationships there is a potential for misunderstanding or for poor advice to be given. But our Creator, in Spirit's perfection and unconditional love for you, will always understand what you are trying to say. Only God knows what is deep within your heart and soul. Only God will give you unconditional love and acceptance and the true answers to all of your questions. Only by developing this deep personal relationship will you truly enjoy the fullness of Spirit's love,

wisdom, insight, and counsel. The growth of this relationship is boundless and increases, over time, in beauty and
glory as human child and Divine Parent unite in a loving
eternal embrace. This is the culmination of the stillness.

Seven Steps of Stillness:

1) Get Physically Relaxed

2) Get Mentally Relaxed

3) Talk to God

4) Ask for Help

5) Give Thanks

6) Listen to God

7) Sense the Divine Presence

6

The Embrace of God

Seeking the stillness and listening to your inner voice will lead you to the happiness and fulfillment you desire. Be patient with this practice, for these rewards come in time. How quickly you reap the benefit depends on how much you can remove the barriers to your receptivity and how willing you are to intuit what your spirit guidance is trying to convey. At first, you may not notice anything different. But one day, you suddenly realize you will seem to be happier overall. Or, you may find that you react more positively in a situation where in the past you became angry or sad. This is your truest indication that you have grown.

As you continue with this practice, your sense of self-worth expands and you find new facets of your personality and ways to better express yourself positively and constructively. New feelings of love will begin to emerge, not only for yourself but for others. You find yourself more willing to share your love. You exhibit more patience, tolerance, generosity, and goodwill toward others as your desire to share God's love tenderly fans the flames of compassion. You find people being drawn to you by the fragrance of love you exude, compelling them to seek the spiritual riches you possess. You will be supremely satisfied to share your treasures with them. All these are your rewards for taking the time to seek the stillness and listen to what your inner spirit strives to convey to you.

Feeling God's Love

God's love is freely and lavishly given to you when you attempt to commune spiritually. Love is the actual inducement to grow in comprehension of spiritual reality. Love produces physical, mental, and spiritual sensory feelings that act as catalysts to heighten your desire for enlightenment. The more love you feel, the more you will crave. Receiving God's love at the physical level feels good; it feels peaceful, it makes you feel whole, it compels you to always want more. God's love is quite addicting, but this addiction produces only beneficial effects, ones that will assist you to become a better person, the person you know deep inside that you were born to be. This is what will lead you to new heights of happiness, joy, and serenity.

These feelings are **real**. They are not just mental exercises or physiological responses. They are your motivation to seek spiritual growth. God's love is like no other feeling you will ever experience. When you sense divine love, when you allow Spirit's love to surround you, you experience a small part of our Creator's divinity. Goodness, mercy, patience, understanding, wisdom – all that is Spirit. The magnitude of the Divine character and the power God commands creates a sense of awe when you are in the flow of our Universal Father/Mother's love; it is humbling and elevating at the same time.

The degree to which you feel this love is proportional to the degree you believe you are worthy. The more you feel loved by God, the more you love yourself and others. This growing feeling of being loved expands your faith that your Spiritual Parent's love will always be there for you whenever you feel alone or lost. Just as a child may run to a loving parent for comfort and consolation when he or she is afraid, so can you turn to your Creator Parent in times of trouble, to receive the understanding and solace you need to buoy you up in the waters of adversity. These spiritual gifts will always be there to answer your cries for help during times of emotional and material crisis.

> Receiving God's love at the physical level feels good; it feels peaceful, it makes you feel whole, it compels you to always want more. God's love is quite addicting, but this addiction produces only beneficial effects, ones that assist you to become a better person, the person you know deep inside that you were born to be.

The Bounties of Listening to Spirit

These blessings are yours for the asking. Ask and you will receive, seek and you will find. But it takes time to see the fruits of your spiritual labor. Discerning spiritual answers is a lifelong pursuit and your capacity to do this increases with conscious cooperation. Trust God to be the true pilot of your ship. Turn your faith, your desires, your aspirations toward your inner spirit and be willing to listen to what it is trying to convey. Often the road is very rough. Many times there are obstacles to surmount. Sometimes these are put in your path deliberately, not to frighten or dishearten you, but to challenge you to bring forth those aspects of your personality that can lead you ever forward to Divinity and to greater awareness of the truth, beauty, and goodness existing in the universe we share with Spirit.

Problems will not miraculously be taken away from you, however, because challenge creates choices. You must decide how to handle your problems. Will you see life as the pursuit of only material goals, or will you allow spirit to add another dimension to your life? When your spirit guides you, you give yourself a great advantage. You avail yourself of the wisdom and counsel God waits to impart to you to help you meet life's obstacles with courage, strength, and hope. Your life's circumstances will not magically change. You will, however, be able to find the means to overcome difficult situations and see them from a different perspective, making them seem less daunting.

Spiritual growth is dynamic, it is stimulating; it is not for the weak or the ease-seeker. If you are up to this challenge, you are given many spiritual gifts and great support to bolster your courage for the long journey to perfection. The greatest barrier to your happiness and spiritual illumination is your unwillingness to move from the chair of complacency, from the clutches of mere existence. If you want to be happy, then you must act! You cannot expect happiness to find you – you must be willing to go out and get it. Only the spirit inspires you to attain the fulfillment you desire. Only the spirit guides you to these rewards. Faith is all you need to attain your goal of happiness. Taking that first step of faith by trusting God's love for you is all your spirit needs to lead you the rest of the way home.

This is the way of spirit. It requires a person to courageously face fears and hopes and sincerely seek to discern the better way to live. Your spirit cannot compel you to do anything against your will. But know this: If you truly want Divine help, it is as close as your mind.

Seek the stillness, practice daily, and these joys will be yours. You will feel God's love for you grow with each passing day. You will gradually become alive with the glow of the divine light that shines from within. Your light is a beacon that illuminates a world lost in darkness. Your light is to be shared, for love cannot live in isolation. This is not its nature. Love exists in relationships and must be shared in its expression. God's love is available for you to internalize, to feel deeply, and then to pass on to those with whom you come into contact.

When you are in love, do you not feel you could burst? Love compels you to jump for joy and to shout to the whole world how wonderful you feel. So it is with God's love – it is not for you to keep inside; it must be shared. As you share love with others, you allow it to grow. Expending that which you have inside allows it to be replenished. That is the nature of love: It never runs out. You never have or give enough love. When you feel you have given it all, more is there for you to draw upon. This is what the Creator has decreed as part of the universal plan. Love is the dominating and driving force of the universe. Love makes you want to do good, not only for yourself but for others. This is the reality of universe. Love dominates. *Love pervades all.*

As you develop this personal relationship with God through your stillness practice, you will be revitalized by the recognition that God does indeed love you; you are a very beloved and very precious child. This security expands your capacity for deep self-acceptance, self-worth, self-love, and true serenity. How could it be other than this? Please realize that you are partaking of Divine Love, the perfect love. When you open to the guidance of your spirit fragment, you access the love that God wishes to share with you. The insight to overcome personal shortcomings, the wisdom to understand who you are, and the courage to be a good and righteous person – plus the desire to serve others with love, kindness, and compassion – are the hallmarks of this developing relationship with Spirit. God's love for you is what allows you to grow in these divine attributes. What is more attractive than to feel the greatest love of all?

> You will feel God's love for you grow with each passing day. You will gradually become alive with the glow of the divine light that shines from within. Your light is a beacon that can illuminate a world lost in darkness.

Section II:
SPIRITUAL ATTITUDES
AND HABITS

Developing your relationship with God through seeking the stillness is the foundation of spiritual growth. The stillness state is key – this is where you communicate with God as the guiding presence in your life and where you actually feel Spirit's love. As this grows, your perspective of spiritual reality broadens and naturally compels you to be loving with people. Other spiritual attitudes and habits can be cultivated to augment your receptivity to spirit. They express your expanding feeling of love: adopting the spiritual attitude of being dependent upon God and altruism, and practicing the spiritual habits of forgiveness, seeing the presence of God in others, prayer, and service.

7

Dependence Upon God

The Divine Parent and human child have a special relationship: It is one of a cooperative, creative undertaking. The Divine Parent instills within the human mind the inner spirit pilot to accompany the child throughout life, and the child gives the Divine Parent the willingness to be led by the divine spirit – alignment with God. In so doing, an innate faith/trust bond is forged between Spirit and human.

This bond allows for two-way communication. The Spirit end is always open and available for contact. However, it is at the human end where the breakdown occurs. Aligning your mind and heart in God, through faith, facilitates your receptivity to hear what God has to say – the answers and support your Divine Parent wants to give you. Dependence upon these answers and guidance foster learning to live the best, Godlike way. It is through time and experience that you incorporate spiritual living into your material life. The more you practice depending upon your inner spirit for guidance and support, the more you begin to sponsor your own sense of independence – being a creative, cooperative child of God in the universal family.

The Experiential Nature of Humans

You were not born knowing how to do things perfectly; you are evolving toward perfection. This presupposes that error is possible, or inevitable. This is the way God has created you – to learn by experience. You cannot escape from your basic nature. Our Creator is so vast and so diverse. The Infinite Personality has created many levels of intelligent life. Among the various levels are celestial beings created in perfection. Perfect beings naturally know and do what is right. On the other hand, there is another level of God's children who have been created to grow progressively by experience according to Spirit's plan and purpose. This is who you are.

There are lessons you need to learn about spiritual reality that sponsors your advancement toward God. Your spirit will lead you to those lessons you are ready to embrace. Trust that when you are truly ready, your divine guide will augment your knowledge with new lessons to advance you to the next level of development. Be patient with this process. It takes time to transform insights into actions – into conscientious behavior. As you are used to more immediate gratification of responses, taking this longer approach to the mastery of your lessons will tax your ability to stay the course. Your inner spirit is the timekeeper; trust that you will stay on track. However, if you do fall short of attaining your lesson the first time, know your spirit will give you the necessary strength and courage to continue. God loves you and wants you to succeed.

Your growth occurs naturally and develops based upon your specific responses to situations. Remember: You are learning by experience. You learn a new concept. Then, it must become a part of your being – it must be internalized before it becomes behavior. It takes time for spiritual experiences to turn into positive and unconscious habits. As your understanding of this truth is nurtured, you also begin to understand the dynamic between knowing the ideal and striving to achieve it. Intellectually, you may comprehend the ideal way to handle a situation, but you may fall short in your ability to react to the situation in the manner you wish. This occurs because at a deeper level the godlike reaction has not taken root in your being. Instead, what happens is the more familiar, but incorrect, response. If you actually had those ideals deeply engrained within your being, they would propel you to act in a different manner.

Accept responsibility for your actions whenever you fall short of attaining your goal, but do not lose sight of the ideal. There are ways to reach the ideal, but the ideal will never be realized if you continue to think ill of yourself, especially if you do not succeed at first. Wallowing in failure instead of seeing your motivation to do right is not the way to develop self-love and self-confidence.

> God's children have been created
> to grow progressively by experience
> according to Spirit's plan and purpose.
> This is who you really are.

Depending on God for Help

Your destiny is to ascend the ladder to perfection step by step through experience. You progressively acquire wisdom and insight to glean the best – the God-given way – on the long road to your perfection destiny. Living in this material realm, you may not have as your eternal goal finding our Creator. However if this were so, your perspective would enable you to view this physical lifetime as only the briefest flicker in the span of eternity. Consequently, your vision of who you are – your comprehension of the truth that you have much to learn and far to grow in your comprehension of universal reality – would afford you the insight to view your life much as you would perceive a toddler discovering the world. Realistically, you cannot be angry with a toddler for not having the wisdom to know what life is all about. Children do not have sufficient life experience to do that. So it is with God. You are the toddler in His universe. Our Creator Parent does not expect you to be perfect or to know all the answers. God does, however, desire you turn to Spirit for the answers. God knows the right way. God is the right way.

You have been influenced by your culture to become self-sustaining and independent. As the human child leaves the cocoon of the home environment to live in the larger world, the parent is hopeful that the child has learned the necessary skills to make his or her own way. Children are schooled in vocational training so they will be able to sustain their materials needs in the workplace, but are they secure in that emotional training that will help them to meet life's disappointments with hope, uncertainty with conviction, intolerance with perseverance, and self-doubt with confidence, and anger with love?

Depending upon God for these spiritual coping skills indicates a non-resistant posture. It is offering your desires to God so that your Divine Parent can give you what is best. It is the direct appeal for what you need – essentially seeking that God's way in your life be done. It is not to say that you are abrogating your will for a slavish robotic approach to living. No! It is the free will offering to be led by a higher, more intelligent Guide that teaches you the insight skills and give you the emotional tools you need to master life successfully so you will progressively become more confident in your own abilities. You will still need to make decisions about your life. But what you yield is your whole-hearted cooperation to be led by Spirit.

Embedded into daily living is the implication that many mistakes will be made because learning by experience entails making choices. Unfortunately, most people have the erroneous notion that they lack the necessary recognition of what is true and right. But God never creates unless Spirit's children are given the proper assistance to master what they need to learn; this assistance comes in the gift of your indwelling spirit. So, if you were to continually look to your inner spirit to assist you to discern truth, you would have much greater insight and guidance. However, most people are unaware of the wonderful gift God has given them. Although help is always available to you, it is your choice to avail yourself of this wonderful guidance.

You will always need to fully experience the lessons your spirit expects you to learn as part of understanding our Creator's ways of universe operation. This is the path to insight and wisdom. The more earnestly and sincerely you

desire to grow in this comprehension, the greater the opportunity your spirit has to help you. Conversely, by not looking
inward and listening to your spirit's voice, you run the risk of
making the same mistakes over and over. Therefore, you suffer the consequences, which sometimes cause great pain,
inner turmoil and despair.

When you suffer shame, guilt, self-deprecation, and
self-doubt due to your errors in judgment and behavior, you
poison your mind with these toxins to the spirit. Yet God
understands your imperfections; He knows why you make
mistakes. He expects you to learn from the mistakes you
make as you experience life one step at a time. Growing in
this way is your nature, do not fight it. It is the fundamental
state of your being. Our Creator Parent is aware of your
attempts to do the right thing. God is aware of the limitations
of your environment, level of intelligence and spiritual
receptivity, and your amount of life experience. Our
Universal Father/Mother knows the motivations within your
heart and mind. You cannot hide from Spirit. Yet you may
fail to realize that God extends His love to you even when
you feel the most confused or unworthy. At those times, God
sees you as a child who has merely stepped off the road to
true happiness. Allow God to guide you back onto the path
to Spirit.

Our Creator is definitely not hiding from you, nor is
He punitive. Our Father/Mother is not waiting for you to sin
so He can deliver a terrible punishment. God is all good, all
loving, all merciful. God cannot be anything less than the
most benevolent, kind, and compassionate Universal
Father/Mother to His children because God is spirit – and
spirit reality is love, truth, beauty and goodness. There is
nothing in God's nature that would make Him want to

punish you. Our Creator's unconditional love constantly flows to you. It is an open connection. But you cut yourself off from God's love when you put up the barriers of self-loathing, doubt and fear.

> Realistically, you cannot be angry with a toddler for not having the wisdom to know what life is all about. Children do not have sufficient life experience to do that. So it is with God. You are the toddler in His universe. Our Creator Parent does not expect you to be perfect or to know all the answers. God does, however, desire you turn to Spirit for the answers. God knows the right way.
> God is the right way.

The Human Feeling of Unworthiness

Within the psyche is a sensing awareness of proportion: the immensity of God contrasted with the human feeling of smallness. This is humility. Healthy self-love, love for others, and love for God results in humbleness – even though you are small and the universe is very large, you know you are important because you are loved. On the other hand, negative self-images yield two forms of expression: false pride (overcompensation) and self-abnegation (self-denial). Both negative aspects of humility are insidious spirit toxins – unworthiness. And most people suffer from some form of unworthiness, born of many experiences.

When you believe that you have problems in life because you are bad or make mistakes and deserve to be punished, or when you have *a belief system about God* that does not support the concept of divine guidance and love, you put up great barriers. Thus, your spirit finds it very difficult to convey its love to you in the form of the solace and comfort you need to overcome negative thinking. Your self-concept and your concepts about God must first be altered if you are to see yourself in a more positive light. Your inner spirit is the wisest guide to help you do this, but you must first be willing to see yourself in a new light. Seeing yourself through the eyes of God enhances this process. Your Father/Mother will give you a new picture of who you are.

Fearful and negative states of mind and emotion inhibit you from feeling God's love, but to God, they are not real. They are spiritual unrealities, and therefore nonexistent at a spiritual level. Yet they create a vast barrier between you and our Universal Father/Mother that sometimes seems insurmountable. Your lack of insight and ability to overcome them because of your feeling of unworthiness has disconnected yourself from Spirit.

You may question why a loving parent would want you to experience some of the difficult circumstances you face. But see yourself as God sees you – as a very small child just beginning eternal life. Poised against the canvas of eternity, life's lessons are the training ground for understanding the true nature of reality. Align your perspective so you can envision your lifetime as extending over the expanse of eternity, throughout which you are always learning deeper meanings of spiritual principles and values. Then, through this insight from your spirit, you will begin to recognize that the mistakes you make here on Earth are merely part of your instruction to awaken you to spiritual reality.

Your mistakes have nothing to do with worthiness. They are merely a teaching mechanism. You are precious, important, and acceptable to our Creator just the way you are. God always loves you and always gives you the necessary assistance to help you learn. If you fear making mistakes and suffering consequences, you simply will not be able to seek the answers. You usually need loving guidance to see the better way. God will help you understand why you must learn by experience, accept your mistakes more gracefully, and judge yourself less harshly.

After making a mistake and experiencing its consequences, you face two choices: continue in the same manner and suffer increasingly severe consequences, or learn another way, a better way. As you choose which path to take, you may eventually glimpse the fact that turning to a higher source to find a better way of living is the spiritual way. This is the way of everything that is true, beautiful, and good. Until you recognize that your life is the reflection of a mind subjected to the limitation of human knowledge and experience, until you exchange your mind for the divine mind by listening to your spirit, until you begin to comprehend that doing things God's way will show you a better method to handle your problems, you will continue to stumble and crash into the pitfalls you have created for yourself.

But even your worst mistakes can be made right with God; you will be given help to overcome them. Our Creator understands all of your shortcomings. You are forgiven every time you falter along the path. God extends His love to you as the supporting hands that pick you up and brush off your bruised ego so you can be on your way. Imagine yourself as a young child trapped inside a hole you were told never to enter. Would your loving mother or father leave you there? Of course not! Our Spiritual Parent is no different. His help would be immediately available the moment you called for help. God understands why you were trapped, and knows all of your motivations. Our Divine Creator would help you to free yourself if you were to ask for Spirit's assistance. Our Universal Father/Mother fully understands why you became ensnared.

God's response to your mistakes illustrates the fundamental principle of mercy. God forgives all, for God knows and understands all. You must never lose sight of Spirit's mercy and compassion, for it is the lifeline that saves you when you are drowning in the pain of your errors. It reconnects you to Divine and Infinite love and allows you to love yourself.

Remember, God's love truly is unconditional. It is never withheld. Your feeling of unworthiness or your beliefs sever your connection. At this time, your perception of yourself through God's eyes will help you connect with yourself as a young child, one who will make countless mistakes for many years to come. You, as this budding spiritual child, are inexperienced. You need compassion and understanding. You crave positive encouragement. When you allow yourself to be absorbed by guilt and self-recrimination, how can you be positively encouraged? The erring young child rushes to the parent for comfort. So should you rush to our Divine Father/Mother for Spirit's understanding and compassion! If you are sincerely sorry for your mistake, you will feel God's mercy extending to you. While you may still have to face the consequences of your actions, the feeling of despair and isolation is gone. God's love and mercy strengthen you to face the consequences. God is by your side to uplift you and to help you endure what you must.

Remember, how you live is conditioned by your environment – the beliefs you were raised with, the ways in which you were treated, and the ideas you developed through your experiences. How can you do things positively if you were raised to learn a negative way? How do children grow into kind and loving adults when they were raised with hatred and anger? Our Creator knows why you act in unkind and negative ways. In spite of this, God still loves and understands you. God knows that beneath this negative behavior lies your potential of perfection, waiting to evolve. Your Spiritual Parent sees beneath the layers of negative thinking and actions. God sees the beauty hiding behind your scars of fear, rejection and mistrust.

See yourself as this embryonic soul, the imperfect child who hungers for perfection. Seeing yourself through the eyes of the spirit enhances your ability to wholeheartedly love and accept yourself as this unique budding spirit, who is still quite the diamond in the rough. The rough edges of ego are polished by the spirit. You are a treasure in the making.

Although your identity can be distorted by the negative effects of error when you align yourself with these toxins to spirit, you can eliminate them by returning to the healing flow of God's love. The positive energy of love expands your God-consciousness and awareness of your identity in our universal family. These are powerful inducements to react with love and goodness to overcome evil. These are the incentives to heighten your sense of self-love and confidence. Accepting God's love is paramount for personal creative expression and self-satisfaction.

Your mistakes have nothing to do with worthiness. They are merely a teaching mechanism. You are precious, important, and acceptable to our Creator just the way you are.

8

Forgiveness

Central to feeling greater self-love is forgiveness. Forgiveness removes the barriers you inflict upon yourselves that inhibit your ability to feel God's love. You may feel unworthy and insignificant because of your imperfect nature. Nevertheless, this is a feeling that separates you from God. Forgiveness affords you the opportunity to return your perspective toward God-consciousness. It helps you realize you are no longer cut off from Divine love because of your mistakes. Once you realize God always loves you and understands why you make mistakes, you re-establish the connection to feeling Spirit's love.

Self-Forgiveness Leads to Self-Love

It becomes much easier to accept forgiveness when you love yourself. You will tend to judge yourself less harshly as you realize the truth of your real identity and your place in the universal family of God. Uplifted by your feelings of self-love, you can acknowledge yourself as a growing child of Spirit, worthy of being loved. This is the foundation of self-forgiveness. Depicting yourself as a child, not only of this world, but as part of a universal family, broadens your perspective so that you view your life as an important part of the fabric of cosmic reality. The confining view that life consists only of physical reality begins to fade as you expand your perception and begin to progress toward a perfect destiny. You will continue to learn and mature as you strive for perfection, and always will you be increasing your capacity to receive and give love.

The errors of your past will gradually fade with the dawning of your realization of a better way to live. You will begin to view your mistakes not with a sense of failure but as a way to learn and grow. As you express your self-love and self-confidence as a child in our Creator's universe, the understanding emerges that – although you must always wrestle with learning through trials and triumphs – always will God be there to help you understand and acknowledge your mistakes. God will give you strength to continue. You will be given courage to face your challenges. You will be given confidence to react with poise, grace, and nobility. You will be given peace to sustain you through your troubles. This, ultimately, liberates you from fear and uncertainty, for you trust and know that Spirit's guidance will never fail you.

You no longer fear decision-making for trust in your Spirit Parent's guidance is steadfast. You are assured that you will be led to the answers and situations that brings you greater understanding about life – especially how to move through life with greater peace, confidence and courage. The shackles of self-doubt, guilt, and shame are broken! This is the exhilaration of self-freedom. You begin to see yourself act more spontaneously in accordance with God's will and law. Most people adhere to restrictive rules and laws to keep their behavior within acceptable standards, but spiritually enlightened individuals are liberated because they do what is right and good naturally. Such people are motivated positively toward experiencing life and its new adventures and challenges; they are assured God will assist them to make the right choices and follow the true path.

Forgiveness, however, is crucial if these blessings are to be yours. Practicing forgiveness while in the stillness state is most effective because you are already in the loving embrace of Spirit, making it easier to ask our Creator to forgive you. God has already forgiven you, but when you ask for forgiveness, you recognize it is you who craves forgiveness from yourself. So, if God really forgives you, how can you not forgive yourself? The majority of your errors and their consequences are due to the lack of insight into spiritual reality and an inability to use your spirit to guide you. If you feel the presence of our Universal Father/Mother's love in your life, if your beliefs support the concept of a loving God, if you accept yourself worthy of Divine love, you readily forgive yourself when you make mistakes. This relieves the tension and guilt from taking yourself too seriously.

If you can do this, you will remove much pressure. You will not place such high expectations upon yourself to perform at some ideal level you may not yet be ready to attain. Let God guide you to new insights to more naturally reach your goals without thwarting your own sense of self-esteem and confidence. As you grow more confident in your ability to follow your spirit's leadings, you gradually see yourself reacting to situations in a positive and Godlike manner. This gentle process of following the spirit's leadings is a more natural way to live, as it does not produce the detrimental stress and tension inherent in the battle of will between your ego and your spirit. Once relieved from this contest, the spirit-led individual is free to experience a wonderful sense of elation – joy!

If you actually had felt the presence of our Universal Father/Mother's love in your life, if your beliefs supported the concept of a loving God, if you accepted yourself worthy of Divine love, you would readily forgive yourself when you make mistakes.

Forgiving Others

There is another component of forgiveness: forgiving others. God freely forgives His children their errors. As our Creator has forgiven you, you must also forgive your brothers and sisters. This precedes giving love to and receiving love from others. Neither you nor your brothers and sisters are perfect. No one has had the ideal environment in which to discern the reality of spiritual values. And the negative actions that have occurred in this world have far-reaching consequences. Therefore, many people suffer for the actions of a few. However, even these erring children are forgiven by God, for Spirit knows what motivates their actions. Our Universal Father/Mothers understands why their actions are not reflective of spiritual values, yet Spirit patiently awaits the time of the spiritual awakening of these errant children. God is patient in waiting for you to become spiritually awakened and asks you to adopt the same perspective.

Practicing forgiveness of others is a vital part of your spiritual development. Forgiving yourself cannot be divorced from loving yourself. Likewise, the added step of forgiving others who have wronged you or your brothers and sisters fosters feelings of love and tolerance for them. The Creator loves all of His children. In God's mercy, He forgives all, for

Spirit knows what is in their hearts and minds. Our Universal Father/Mother sees you on the road evolving toward perfection, and so are your brothers and sisters. Some may have further to grow, however, since their actions reflect fear and other negative emotions. Nevertheless, see this as indicating that God's love is absolutely paramount for healing their inner wounds. As you learn to love yourself more, as you become more aware of your evolving spiritual potential, you will understand the significance of your experiential nature. You will begin to recognize that you are not expected to be perfect yet. This is true for your brothers and sisters as well.

> Many people suffer for the actions of a few. However, even these erring children are forgiven by God.

Understanding Others' Negative Actions

No one has the benefit of a perfect upbringing. Everyone learns through experience, everyone makes mistakes. The correction of mistakes is punishment-oriented in your society, and regularly produce the opposite effect in understanding and especially behavior. Consequently, some people make more mistakes and act more negatively than others because the gentle balm of teaching a better way has not been applied. While you must judge actions, and society has every right to impose judgments upon actions deemed to be detrimental, you as an individual should not judge your brothers' and sisters' spiritual status. You do not know what compels them to commit evil; you do not truly understand their real motivations. What forgiving others means is: Separating the person from their actions. This is the meaning of loving the sinner but hating the sin. You do not condone their wrong actions, but you try to see them as God sees them. You learn to forgive them as our Creator does. *Spirit knows why they have erred.* Our Universal Father/Mother understands their sorrow and inner turmoil, yet they are still loved and forgiven. Likewise, it is your responsibility to freely forgive as well. But know this: *your ability to forgive others is directly proportional to the degree you will advance spiritually.*

By practicing forgiveness you are afforded the opportunity to better understand both the shortcomings and the potential of being human. All people struggle in their search to understand life. Some people are unaware of true reality by their ungodlike actions, but they are still God's children. You do not truly nor fully understand the nature of spiritual reality. If you did, you would behave and live differently.

Unkind words, thoughts and, especially actions, testify to the fact your ways are not much further evolved than those of children. Your ideas and ways of communication may be more sophisticated, but your actions of selfishness and greed, anger and hatred, intolerance and cruelty are exactly expressive of the immature ways of children. Envision a group of very young children playing and hear their petty quarrels. Now think of a group of adults arguing and realize that the dynamic is still the same though the ramifications are on a much greater scale. Understand that a child of three or four has not yet developed the insight to be aware of the hateful, hurtful things they say. Likewise for adults: You say hateful and unkind words like these children, but you do not fully realize the repercussions of your actions, their impact on others, and their effects on deeper spiritual levels.

So it is with your less spiritually developed brothers and sisters. You must understand that they truly are just small children too, grasping in the darkness, blind to the spiritual light that illuminates the path to true happiness and joy. Feel compassion for them, even when they commit acts of hatred. Forgiving their shortcomings helps you to see they have farther to go along their path; that they are still sleeping spiritually. God loves them, and they have inner spirits; they simply are unaware, and their actions attest to this fact.

This is a difficult concept to accept initially, especially when you see people leading evil lives and committing barbarous acts. However, if you could look inside their minds and understand the depths of their unhappiness and inner pain, you would feel more compassion for them. These people are truly pathetic. *They actually do not realize what they are doing.* They are oblivious to the spiritual component of their identity and the deeper impact of their actions. While forgiveness does not mean you should allow them free rein to commit evil because you feel compassion for them, it does mean that you, as a more spiritually enlightened individual, must look at them through God's eyes and see them as truly lost. They desperately need to feel the healing power of our Creator's love. It would be their initiation to a happier life. To the extent you can, share love with them. Try to show them a better way. Help them to see the joy of spiritual living by your positive actions.

Understand that a child of three or four has not yet developed the insight to be aware of the hateful, hurtful things they say. Likewise for adults: You say hateful and unkind words like these children, but you do not fully realize the repercussions of your actions, their impact on others, and their effects on deeper spiritual levels.

Importance of Forgiveness
for Growing Spiritually

Understand that it is your own choices that determine how closely you align yourself with spiritual reality. How you treat people and react to them is a conscious decision on your part. Your insight into and actual comprehension of spiritual reality is reflected by your responses to others. Although you cannot control another person's actions toward you, you can control your own reactions toward them. When you forgive someone for their unwise or evil actions, you stay connected to the spiritual energy of God's love to help you overcome the negative consequences of what they have done to you. Forgiving them will help you to stay focused on the positive emotions you need to keep yourself protected against their evil. If you are courageous enough to do this, you overcome great injustice and despair – you triumph because you are supported by the greatest power in heaven and earth, God.

You will be given strength, comfort, support, understanding, hope, and above all, love. This spiritual clothing has the power to vanquish all evil, but first allow yourself to be protected from the negative actions of others. Only forgiveness offers the release of the tension of resentment and anger which hardens your heart and mind against acting positively toward them. The positive response you show to them by your actions will be registered upon their minds *and may be a great inducement and inspiration for them to change their behavior.*

This perspective of forgiveness is fundamental to building your capacity to love. When you view people as needing God's love, it makes forgiveness just a little easier.

Although people still must suffer the consequences of their actions and must live up to the repercussions of their wrong-doing, recognize that it is your responsibility to acknowledge them as God's child – your brother or sister. Unfortunately, they may be so far removed from our Creator's love that they cannot begin to grasp that God loves and wants them to experience the joys of living in Spirit's family. They cannot feel this love and joy because of great pain, so they continue on a path of evil. Indeed, this is very sad. Reacting with resentment and anger only continues the chain reaction of negative behavior, driving deeper wedges between you and God, you and the other person, and you and your ability to love yourself.

Actions do speak louder than words. When you forgive, **God's love and a sense of freedom from the bondage of negative emotions comes your way many times over.** It fills you with happiness and helps you to act more positively. Another person seeing this love and forgiveness in action may be compelled to seek what you have.

The truly great person is one who helps others awaken to God's love by individual acts of goodness. This person is performing the highest universe service of aiding another person to find God.

In the act of forgiving others for their misdeeds, you allow yourself the opportunity for greater insight into their motivations and behavior. Understanding why someone acts in a certain way kindles feelings of compassion for them. And if you allow compassion the fullest range of expression, love begins to bloom. This is why forgiveness is vital to spiritual growth and to universal functioning. Forgiveness ultimately grows love if it is tended by a sincere heart and allowed to blossom to the fullest extent. When you feel love for one another, you accept the fact God loves them, that they have an inner spirit. The sooner you realize and practice this, the faster will your world be healed of its evil. There is no room within God's family for anything but love, tolerance, compassion, kindness, patience, understanding, truth, beauty, and goodness.

Forgiveness leads to understanding, understanding leads to compassion and compassion to love. In loving and forgiving your brothers and sisters, as well as yourself, you allow your inner spirit free rein to better communicate its truths to you, free from the toxins that inhibit health and happiness.

> The truly great person is one who helps others awaken to God's love by their individual acts of goodness. This person is performing the highest universe service of aiding another person to find God.

9

Seeing the Presence
of God in Others

Developing the spiritual habit of seeing the presence of God
in others and recognizing that all are equally worthy of God's
love is the natural repercussion and acceptance of our God-
given personality.

Everyone Is a Child of God

It is in the stillness that you build your connection with
God's love. As you grow in self-love and self-acceptance, at
some point the insight will arise that all individuals develop
spiritually, although at different rates. People are at various
stages of maturity. Some individuals may be more spiritually
enlightened than others – they may seek spiritual growth as
their life's goal. Some may not have yet awakened to the call
of their inner spirit. Just the same, God loves them and is
waiting for their time of awakening to the greater reality existing beyond their current level of understanding. Spiritual
development requires the acknowledgment of the spiritual
potential within your brothers and sisters, even though it may

be dormant. Rejoice in the genuine truth that our Creator loves them. This is the acceptance of the family of God – the fraternity of humanity.

Your capacity for spiritual development broadens when you accept that God loves each individual. Seeing another person as a brother or sister in our universal family fosters the fruits of tolerance, compassion, cooperation, and understanding; it provides the fertile soil from which altruism springs. Cultivating these fruits of the spirit leads you to act more positively with people, and fosters open communication between you and your spirit. Your growth into God-consciousness gently yields the recognition of your kinship with all of creation, particularly with the family of humanity. And this leads you to embrace expanded concepts of what it means to live as a member of God's family. The awareness of every living being as the expression of our Creator's love is one that will continually unfold in your mind and in your experience of your brothers and sisters; growing to love and serve them is one of the greatest lessons you **must master** to progress spiritually.

Love is the driving force/energy that God creates to bind all creation to Him. You and your brothers and sisters are moving toward Spirit. Our Creator's love lives in each of you to guide you to godward. When you see the presence of God in others, you recognize the spirit within everyone. You no longer view yourself as separate or isolated from your brothers and sisters but as a part of them, for you have a common bond: You come from the same Divine Parent. The spirit presence of our Universal Father/Mother in each evolving child weaves this family into a tightly knit fabric of universal love and cosmic kinship. In God there is unity. Recognizing that unity diminishes all feelings of alienation, intolerance, prejudice and bigotry. Human beings all differ intellectually, physically, socially, racially, and culturally, but at the spiritual level you are all equal. You have the God-given gift of your unique personality and the creativity to express it in your approach to and perception of Divine Spirit.

No one person has the only one correct way to find the Creator. The diversity of God's personality has brought into being many varieties of intelligent life, all of whom are an expression of the Divine Being. ***You are a unique revelation of our Creator's love.*** Your true identity reveals a unique dimension of Divinity. When you reflect the spiritual values of truth, beauty, and goodness, you express the Supreme Being in a new and matchless way. The thread of your personality is woven into the tapestry of the universe, adding greater beauty and richness to the expanding design. God is forever expanding, enhancing, and perfecting this design by adding the myriad colorful threads of the personality through the creative process.

This may be a bit difficult to fully appreciate at first glance. Many times people think they have found the one correct interpretation of God. This is unfortunate, for such a singular perspective sows the seeds of intolerance. The truth that harvests the fruits of acceptance, tolerance, and understanding is: Each child is loved equally by God and each person reflects our Creator's love. Therefore, to see the Spirit's presence in another, at first, requires frequent conscious readjustment because the usual way of seeing them is based upon your perceptions and experiences. Your yardstick for measuring another person's worth or assessing their spiritual status may discount the fact they differ in opinions, cultures, and habits. But are they really so different from you? Do they not still experience the very same feelings as you? All people share the same spirit reality; they are all indwelt by a spirit fragment and are loved equally by God. How can you begin to recognize and believe this?

To foster this truth, you need to develop the habit of seeing the spiritual light in others. To truly believe that your brothers and sisters are children of the Universal Father/Mother, this thought must become alive within your mind and felt within your heart. This requires a continual realignment of your perception of others until this perspective becomes an automatic reaction. There may be many blocks preventing you from seeing others as children of God. It can be very difficult to look beyond someone's negative actions, especially when you judge them as being evil and deserving of punishment. Or you may believe that a person needs to behave a certain way or believe in certain concepts before he or she is worthy of God's love. These attitudes must be removed for your heart to open to the flow of God's love and the anger, intolerance, and other spirit poisons that inhibit you from seeing the Spirit presence in your brothers and sisters can be washed away.

Seeking the stillness affords your spirit the opportunity to awaken you to this cosmic awareness and responsibility. With increasing clarity and understanding, acknowledging your brothers' and sisters' spiritual kinship comes into focus as you commune with God and feel His love. As your spirit communicates this truth to your mind, you will gradually recognize how our Creator entwines and enfolds all humanity in infinite love and mercy. This concept unlocks the door to the whole cosmos. Not only are you a citizen of a country or of a given planet, you are a universal citizen – a member of the family of God. You are welcome to partake of the privileges and responsibilities accompanying living in this universal family. *The greatest responsibility you have as a citizen of the universe is to love others with the love God has bestowed upon you.* Your happiness will know no bounds when you share this love with them.

Communion with God in stillness, seeking forgiveness, and seeing the presence of God in others are three lessons to practice daily if you wish to accelerate your spiritual progress. These are very effective ways to increase your capacity for self-love and to share love with others. If you want to experience bountiful love and peace, these are the habits to master. Love is the universal panacea. It is the great healer. It will heal you. Over time and if practiced by enough people, it will heal your world.

In God there is unity. Recognizing that unity diminishes feelings of alienation, intolerance, prejudice and bigotry. Human beings differ intellectually, physically, socially, racially, and culturally, but at the spiritual level you are all equal.

Learning to Love Others – Tolerance

It may seem daunting to think you must love everyone the same way that God loves you. The challenge of spiritual mastery is not to deter you from trying your best to practice seeing the spirit in others. This is the goal. It is the *ideal* for which to strive. However, there are practical ways to begin to see others in a different light and to react to them in a positive manner. It is natural to want to love others more every day; however, it is unrealistic to feel about acquaintances or strangers the same way you feel about family and friends. Take small steps toward the ideal instead of trying to intellectually manufacture a belief system that may not house genuine feelings of love.

How, then, to take these small steps demonstrating love? Love is shown in many ways – through compassion, tolerance, kindness, patience to others. By choosing to react to people with these positive qualities over time your choices build a habit. Eventually your behavior naturally becomes dominated by love. Imagine yourself in a situation with a person who tries your patience – perhaps a situation where you have previously lost your temper with them. Stop. Ask God for patience and kindness. Ask for whatever spiritual coping tool you need. When you feel you have received what you need, then respond to that person. If instead of losing your temper you reply in a kind and gentle manner, wouldn't this be a way to share love? Do you think they, in turn, would respond to you differently? It is better to be gentle than abrasive. Doesn't this produce better results? Don't you feel better when you react in a loving manner? Know this: God will give you everything you need to act positively. You, however, must remember to ask for it.

If you saw Jesus crossing the street struggling with a heavy burden, would you not rush to his side to help him? Envision your brothers and sisters as if they were Jesus. You would naturally want to do whatever you could for Jesus. So it is with your brothers and sisters. In them lives a part of God. Although their actions may not reflect their spirituality and you may not see it, nonetheless it is there. Respond to that person as if you were speaking to their spirit – as if you were speaking directly to our Father/Mother. Treat them with the love, dignity, and respect you would if you were standing in the presence of God. In reality, you are. Whatever you do to others, you do to God. Honor their divine inner spirit by treating them with kindness. This, in turn, allows your spirit to communicate with theirs.

When you react to your brothers and sisters in this loving manner, when you respect their spirit, you do more good than you realize. You give their spirit fragment a more fertile environment for imparting its leadings to their minds. Eventually, this act of kindness will be registered in their consciousness, and one day they may feel compelled to reciprocate – if not with you, with someone else.

> React to that person as if you were speaking to their spirit – as if you were speaking directly to our Father/Mother. Treat them with the love, dignity, and respect you would if you were standing in the presence of God. In reality, you are.

Practicing Tolerance

Seeing the presence of God in others is one of the goals and ideals for growing your character. This sensitivity is very difficult to master, and you certainly do not have to become perfect at it. You have eternity to accomplish this. But what is expected of you during your lifetime in the physical domain is to awaken to the truth that you and your brothers and sisters have this living spirit within. Recognize that spirit. Follow it. And most important, learn to love it. Respect it in your brothers and sisters. It is their link to God.

At your level of experience, you will not always love everyone equally or with the same intensity of feeling. Furthermore, you may not wish to associate with some people because of their unlovely actions. This is your choice and it is perfectly acceptable. Nevertheless, it is important to react to them in a positive way, for it is your responsibility as a child of God's family to treat everyone in a kind and respectful manner. The only person's behavior and thinking you can control is your own. Let God be concerned about other people's thoughts and actions; let their spirits work within them. **Master yourself.** As a member of the cosmic family, you contribute to the unfolding of God's beneficent purpose for the universe when you take this approach in interacting with your brothers and sisters.

If you can treat people with common courtesy but cannot respond lovingly, this is still better than responding with anger or hatred. If the best you can do is to look with compassion at a person who shows you anger, that is better than returning a similar negative response. When you look at a person and see them in a positive light, this is better than assuming the worst about him or her. If this is the best you can do, because you cannot feel a deeper sense of acceptance or because you may not wish to associate with him or her, then so be it. Keep in mind that these responses are positive and indicate steps toward spiritual maturity. Remember that growth even in small measures is still growth. What is important is that you are deepening your spirituality, you are learning to love more. This is what God expects of you – that you continue to try.

Do not anticipate that you will love everyone instantly because you believe it is the right thing to do. The feelings that condition your behavior truly reveal how much you love your fellows. You may wish to love everyone and know it is the right thing to do, but if you do not actually feel that love alive inside you, how can you realistically expect to depict this in your actions with others? If your altruistic feelings and behavior have not been fully integrated, then you will disappoint yourself. So repeats the cycle of self-recrimination and guilt. You feel unworthy of love and cuts yourself off from feeling God's love. This is dangerous; it causes greater inner turmoil and distracts from the spiritual growth you are trying to achieve.

To cultivate tolerance, it can be helpful to view people from a different vantage point. Adopting the perspective of your brothers and sisters as little children in large bodies will foster a spiritual attitude toward them. Envision them as a three- or four-year-old. Look into their eyes and see the hope, wonderment, love – all of the potential that exists in the eyes of a young child. Everyone has this potential; the same essence living within a young child is still there. Look beyond their physical presence to discern this essence living in your brothers and sisters. The natural tendency would be to react to them with the same compassion, tenderness, and consideration with which you would treat a young child. Within everyone is a spirit longing for love, companionship, beauty – for all good things life has to offer. Seeing this light in your brothers and sisters is seeing the presence of God within them.

Most people truly try to lead good lives. Their actions may attest to the fact they have yet to awaken to the call of their spirit fragment, but usually they are motivated by their understanding of what they believe is right. It can be very difficult to know the correct or best way to live when the truest guide, which lives inside, is not allowed to reveal this. Most people turn to external sources for guidance. Theology, philosophy, and psychology which have been developed through the limitations of human thinking may provide them with only the rudiments of truth. Although it happens unintentionally, people may be led down a wrong path. It is little wonder so many live in darkness on this world! They have not yet seen the light of truth living within each person's mind, the light that leads to the correct way of living and unfolds the great mysteries of life. As a spiritually alive individual, let your light shine on them to guide them to the answers they seek.

> When you look at a person and see them in a positive light, this is better than assuming the worst about him or her. Keep in mind these responses are positive and they indicate steps toward spiritual maturity.

10

Altruism and Service

For some people spiritual growth may seem so unattainable because they linger in the darkness of their own experiences and limited thinking. They become disheartened by their failed attempts to do good and may feel unworthy due to their shortcomings. Instead of seeking the guidance of their spirit, they wallow in emotions of self-deprecation, guilt, shame, and remorse. They cannot persevere because they do not know where to find the strength to continue. These attitudes swell and can turn into bitterness, anger, and even hate, discoloring actions toward others.

Helping Others Overcome
Their Spiritual Blocks

Struggles will prevail until people open to their spirit's guidance. The presence of God is in them and sits poised to help them. But they may not yet be ready to listen. You can help them overcome these negative attitudes and actions by showing God's love through your compassion and understanding. Guide them to the better action by sharing your love with them, even when they treat you unjustly. This is the example

Jesus set when he taught to return good for evil. Even a small amount of good has the power to overcome great evil. React to your brothers and sisters positively. You will be amazed at the results. You are giving their spirit an opportunity to register something of spiritual value. This highly significant contribution you offer your brothers and sisters is activated by altruism.

Recognizing the light of spirit within your spiritual siblings triggers this response. You tolerate others' opinions, for example, because you acknowledge everyone's God-given right to expression. Even though you may disagree, you more naturally begin to respect another's views because you understand them to be their honest outlook on life. You respect their perspective similarly to how you would see a young child who does not have the advantage of wider experience. It is acceptable to disagree with others. Within the principal of altruism is the innate recognition that each person has the right to express their God-given individuality. No two people will ever see everything exactly the same way. You cannot condemn people for this, for that is an expression of the Creator's diversity of personality. But God loves each and every one of His children exactly the same way. Conflicts will arise since no two people are alike; you will never fully understand or appreciate another's motivations. The altruistic attitude sponsors your view of their status as our Universal Father/Mother's son and daughter and gives you the signal to love them for their unique expression of personality. It allows you to accept them for the individuals God has created them to be.

On a world where so much evil exists, it can be difficult to always recognize the spirit presence in some individuals because of their ungodlike actions. While avoiding association with them is a personal prerogative, it is truly your responsibility as a son or daughter of the loving Universal Father/Mother to recognize their status as children of God. Your comprehension of this may be more on an intellectual level, however, so putting it into practice and living it will be much more challenging.

Seeking the stillness underscores your ability to help others because it is truly the best way to feel how much our Creator loves you. And how it motivates you to love others! It is fundamental for forgiving yourself and others. Love negates the pain people feel due to their ungodlike actions. Also, it yields another important perspective – it separates the action from the individual. You may hate the deeds people commit, but if you really understood why people do such evil things, you would feel compassion for them. This understanding can only be realized by the conscious recognition that they are children of God. Our Divine Creator sees the negative action, but still loves the child. Ask your spirit to adjust your thinking to hate the sin but love the sinner. This lesson is one you will continually practice throughout life. Mastering it can be very difficult, but you can begin to change your attitude to embrace a more spiritually enlightened outlook by turning to Father/Mother and asking to see others through Divine eyes.

> On a world where so much evil exists, it can be difficult to always recognize the spirit presence in some individuals because of their ungodlike actions. While avoiding association with them is a personal prerogative, it is truly your responsibility as a son or daughter of the loving Universal Father/Mother to recognize their status as children of God.

Altruism Leads to Service

The practices of forgiveness and seeing the presence of God in your less spiritually mature brothers and sisters are difficult to separate for they are mutually interdependent. The more you forgive your siblings for their faults, the more you appreciate them as being equally loved by God. These are the younger members of our universal family. And what is the dynamic of healthy families? There must be harmony and cooperation for them to function properly. Unique personalities are cooperative only when their characters are coordinated into a unified whole by a strong and loving guiding force. Harmony is cultivated by tolerance, acceptance, patience, understanding, compassion, mercy, and generous doses of forgiveness. Living this spiritual principle is what grows love. Love is what keeps families together even when some members act in most unlovely ways. Drawing upon the love of our Father/Mother will keep this perspective foremost in your mind and heart.

The more love you feel, the greater your capacity to give love. You can live in a flow of love, receiving and sharing, inhaling love and exhaling it in all you do, all the while transforming yourself in this ebb and flow. As you develop these spiritual habits and incorporate them into your daily routine, the outcome will bring you an expansive, boundless joy. Spiritual living is like this – it brings feelings of peace and happiness beyond your ability to express in words. However, to truly reap the full benefit of these desirable and attainable feelings, the attitude of altruism – the uplifting inner sense of selflessness – will heighten your appreciation and give you greater peace and happiness. As you sense these feelings, offer them to our Father/Mother and ask how you can help others to feel this love for their own.

This is a joyful undertaking. Bringing love and goodness to another person is the highest joy of spiritual living; it is the greatest service you can perform for another. Altruism is the springboard for service, but the altruistic attitude needs to carefully cultivated so it can yield the greatest fruit. Self-centered persons cannot grow spiritually because their sense of self-importance is magnified. Selfishness inflates the ego and creates isolation from others. However, when you help your brothers and sisters in whatever manner, whether it is for one or many, you diminish your self-importance. You no longer view yourself as better than others, and their well-being becomes important to you. When you act for another's benefit, whether or not you recognize the deeper meaning behind your action, you are acting spiritually.

View love as the desire to do good to others. Service is love in action. The service-motivated individual spontaneously acts out of a desire to do good for others. There is nothing self-seeking about it; you simply acknowledge that another person's welfare is as important as your own. You recognize that others have just as much purpose and value as you; which is the essence of seeing the presence of God in others. Acts of service and kindness do not have to be large; even if you just smile at someone, you show kindness. You are acting according to real spiritual values. You are sharing God's greatest gift – love.

> Bringing love and goodness to another person is the highest joy of spiritual living; it is the greatest service you can perform for another.

Service Is Integral to Spiritual Growth

Performing acts of service elevates seeing the presence of God in others to the next level of spiritual development. Service is not a slavish duty-bound commitment done out of obligation. Service is the free-will choice to express the joy of living in order to help motivate others to participate in the glory of living in God's family. Service is best expressed in your attitude – your desire – to help others. This is what is important to Spirit, not some lofty ideal that you imagine you must perform at some elevated level. There are significant meanings behind every action, thought, and impulse. The unselfish act of giving, however small a particular action may seem to you, registers universal principles of love and goodness onto the minds of both giver and recipient. The goodness of the action is appreciated by the receiver and is reflected in the giver. The beauty of the relationship forged between the two individuals is a new expression of God's infinite love.

You will sense this love in your being. This is actually physiologically registered in your body. Helping another brings a sense of well-being, peace, happiness, and fulfillment. Why is this so? These beautiful feelings exist because God has created them to inspire and motivate His children to act according to spiritual values. Doing something that makes you feel good compels you to continue. This is what positively motivates you to perform acts of kindness and service. When your actions naturally propel you to continue to spontaneously do good to others, then you will see in yourself a spiritually fragrant individual. This transformed individual is a responsible cosmic citizen, one who is ready to accept the challenges and joys of living a spiritually enriched life, a life blessed with the treasures of peace, confidence, integrity, courage and grace.

What is more satisfying than this? Understand how these very small steps can lead you to such satisfying rewards. Do not think that because you cannot save the entire world, you cannot have an impact. You do. You make an impact when you show even the smallest kindness. It has a reverberating ripple-like effect. You do not know how much your help means to someone. Showing kindness to others will inspire them to do the same to someone else; they will act generously with others, and so on. This is what will change your world.

This kind of service is the deeper meaning of seeing the presence of God in others. It is fundamental to your continued spiritual development and the enlightenment of your society. Each person contributes to the fabric of civilization. How much goodness do you wish to donate to the world? How inspired are you to help improve the condition of your planet?

You shall be known by your actions. The great person is the one who is truly good. Goodness is developed by practicing acts of kindness daily, by seeing that your brothers and sisters are as beloved by our Creator as you are. Feel God's love reverberate in your life. Share this love with others. Be motivated by your inner spirit. Reflect true spiritual values. This is the signature of a great and noble character.

> Do not think that because you cannot save the entire world, you cannot have an impact. You do. You make an impact when you show even the smallest kindness.

11

Prayer

The true value of prayer is underappreciated on this world; therefore, prayer tends to be underused and misunderstood. Often you turn to prayer as a petition for help in dire times – when you or your loved ones are ill, when your lives take a turn for the worse and you do not know where else to turn, or when your lives may be physically endangered. It is wise to turn to prayer during these times; however, if you do not resort to it other times, it may be because you do not fully understand its true purpose. Prayer delivers your willingness to let Spirit intercede into the situation and influence it according to God's desires and plans.

In a natural progression, spiritual attitudes foster spiritual habits. The foundation of spiritual growth is seeking the stillness, which instills greater self-love and self-acceptance by opening the valve to receiving God's love. Forgiveness removes the barriers of guilt, unworthiness, and shame, and also serves to replace feelings of anger and intolerance toward others with those of compassion and understanding. Seeing the presence of God in others takes forgiveness to the next level by elevating your brothers and sisters to the status of children of God, which leads you to want to do good for them. Service is the natural expression of that desire. One of the most effective spiritual services you can perform is to pray for others. Prayer acts as the catalyst to spiritually uplift another person. It is the spiritual habit that best exemplifies one's desire to serve, a spiritual habit that we learn to master as we move toward God-consciousness.

As you grow in feeling God's love, as you develop love and compassion for your brothers and sisters, your desire to help others will become more pronounced. Although praying for yourself can augment your own development, especially when spiritual gifts such as patience and understanding are sincerely sought, prayer becomes most beneficial when it is used to help another understand that he or she is a beloved child of a tender, merciful Spiritual Parent. The sincere desire to help someone gain greater insight and wisdom into his or her relationship with God is the supreme joy of spiritual living. This is the most loving and selfless service you can perform for another.

> Prayer is the delivery of your willingness to let Spirit intercede into the situation and influence it according to God's desires and plans.

How Prayer Works

A vast spiritual circuitry has been put in place. It is a complex interlacing of spiritual, mindal, and physical energies whose purpose is to transmit the love God has bestowed for administering the universe. This circuitry touches every one of our Universal Father/Mother's children. These energies are used by many different spiritual beings, beautiful celestial helpers who assist our Creator in carrying out the plan of organization and function in a universe dominated by love. Prayer is one of the communication methods the Divine Creator employs to help all beings awaken to the joys of spiritual living. It is a most effective means of awakening them to the truth, beauty, and goodness of living in God's family.

Free will is the foundation of an individual's path, but prayer facilitates one's receptivity to the higher influences. Prayer emits a specific energy in the form of a subtle pressure, or impression, upon your mind. Gradually, as the spiritual impression or sensing becomes stronger in one's conscious mind, the prayer recipient may become aware of a gentle urge or small voice that leads toward a specific and positive direction.

Thus, the spiritual energy that you send to another person through prayer is one way you can cooperate with celestial friends to help your earthly brothers and sisters. Prayer assists spiritual beings to perform the functions for which they were created. The celestials take the prayer and instill what it wants to accomplish onto the higher levels of consciousness of the human recipient. However, the time when the individual is ready to benefit from the petition must be awaited; that time is the point when the new thought is actually ready to dawn in the conscious mind of the prayer recipient.

You are surrounded by many friendly celestial beings and spiritual energies. You have angels charged with your watchcare, who cooperate with your inner spirit to help you learn various lessons. Your indwelling spirit also tries to impart certain spiritual lessons to you. However, you may not yet be ready to listen. Angels may step in at this point to create those conditions in your life that will help you to awaken to spiritual reality. They work diligently behind the scenes of your life, to some extent arranging the situations where you have to choose which road to take – the easier way of least resistance or the rugged spiritual path that enables you to recognize those spiritual values and principles that lead you to a greater love for God, self, and your brothers and sisters.

Your angels are not necessarily here to make life easy for you. Although they may or may not protect you in certain life-threatening situations, their main function is to help you master certain spiritual concepts. They endeavor to develop your potential as a child of our Creator. How? By urging you to overcome the difficulties of daily living through meeting your problems with the perspective of spiritual insight and understanding. Unbeknownst to you, they encourage you to embrace the challenges and opportunities they place in your path. They try to accomplish this with the oversight of your indwelling spirit fragment. God knows the best path for you; Spirit employs many celestial helpers to assist your spirit growth. The beautiful synchrony of the Universal Father/Mother and spiritual helpers in assisting the children of the evolutionary worlds to gain enlightenment is harmonized by prayer.

While you may certainly pray for yourself, it is truly unnecessary, for our Universal Father/Mother knows of your every need, even before you realize it. However, you may certainly pray for yourself if it brings you closer to God or gives you a sense of comfort. Prayer for yourself could be considered communication between you and your Creator. This is what communion in the stillness state accomplishes: It develops your relationship with God; you grow in comprehension of spiritual reality and what it means to live in the universe as a child of God. In addition, your inner spirit reveals what will help you to master living, what tools you truly need to be successful. This divine guide leads you step by step, progressing through the mazes and minefields of daily life, helping you to circumvent the traps by giving you the insight and skills you need to deftly maneuver around them. Prayer for yourself, therefore, becomes that two-way communication – your spirit is actively spurring you toward enlightenment when you commune with God in the stillness. Your future growth is assured; your mastery of living is underway.

> Prayer is one of the communication methods the Divine Creator employs to help all beings awaken to the joys of spiritual living. It is a most effective means of applying spiritual pressure on a person to awaken him or her to the truth, beauty, and goodness of living in God's family.

Effective Prayer

Prayer is best directed toward others. Your unselfish intention to help another elevates a simple heartfelt desire to the more meaningful level of spiritual reality – service. Any time you help others, you share love, you share the love of our Divine Creator – you perform a significant spiritual service. Prayer is an alignment with spiritual reality, and thus it is important to understand how prayer can be best used. There are two essential components of prayer. In order to be truly effective, it must be sincere and it should be specific.

The unselfish urge to help another person comprises the sincerity component of prayer. Love is the desire to do good to others. When you pray for others, you seek their edification, what is best for them. This is the goal. Sincerity of motivation drives the prayer petitioner to ask that the best be done for the recipient. *You may not always know what another person's highest good might be, but the sincerity that underscores your petition and the feeling of love motivating your prayer is of utmost importance.* God sees into your heart and knows when you are sincere. He knows when you truly wish to help your brothers and sisters. Our Creator desires to put your intention to serve to good use. The fundamental ingredients of sincerity necessary for spiritual agencies to assist a person are twofold: the love you feel for the prayer recipient and your intention to help that individual.

Your comprehension of the two elements of effective prayer can make composition of the petition easier and more meaningful. The other component of effective prayer is to seek a specific outcome. The likelihood that the prayer will be answered is enhanced when you seek a spiritual outcome allowing the person's spirit to register truth on their mind. Both components are equally important, but, in order for the component of specificity of outcome to be effective, thought and insight into what the individual truly needs most is required. This may take some reflection on your part.

Imagine yourself in a family situation where your spouse and your child are not getting along. Perhaps this parent would lose patience with the child and react angrily. If you were to pray, "God bless my family," what exactly could the spiritual agencies overseeing your family do to help your spouse overcome the problem? An example of an effective prayer, then, might be, "Father, help my spouse understand that losing patience with and lashing out at our child is not an effective disciplinary measure."

What may happen after the prayer is offered is this: A situation might be created for the parent to realize that losing his or her temper only exacerbates the problem. The parent might then be on the receiving end of anger from a coworker or another person. In that circumstance, he or she may realize that the anger creates more harm than good, which might yield the realization into the situation with the child. Or a mental impression could emerge that forms the same thought, leading the parent to a new and positive measure to deal with the child. In time, insights of specific ways to better handle the situation will take shape in this person's conscious mind. Identifying and comprehending a positive outcome, through insight, is what most helps people to change their behavior.

Another example of specific prayer is to think about what a friend or family member might need in his or her life to overcome emotion or material-related problems. Perhaps this person is faced with financial difficulties and is very anxious about the future. An effective prayer would be one that provides insight into ways to help surmount the problem, and/or to request that the individual be given strength, courage, and hope to see him or her through the difficult time. Remember: There is always a spiritual antidote to every negative emotion and behavior people exhibit due to their life challenges. Effective prayer identifies the antidote that most efficiently assists the person through the obstacle.

Praying for a specific outcome allows certain celestial agencies to cultivate conditions in the mind of the individual or to create a situation that leads a person to ascertain the answers. Either a situation will be developed that allows them to more fully understand the harmful consequences of their actions, or a particular thought will emerge to stimulate the aspiration to find a better way. When this occurs, then conditions are fertile within the mind to implant the spiritual, correct way to handle the situation. Prayer used effectively is a powerful force to make dramatic changes.

Prayerful humans and celestial beings can cooperate to evoke changes in negative attitudes and behavior. The harmonious spiritual circuitry of the universe works toward the upliftment of humanity. It facilitates the action of the celestials and receptivity of the prayer recipient. Your participation in this upliftment effort is more beneficial than you realize. You contribute more love into the universe, thus expanding God's purpose and plan. On a personal level, you may feel a sense of renewal and satisfaction, which will augment your desire to continue to help others. You may find prayer becoming more naturally incorporated into your day as you sense your increasing desire to contribute to the edification and happiness of your brothers and sisters. The truly great and heroic person is the one who works toward the betterment of humanity and society.

Be mindful that the outcome of the prayer needs to be of *spiritual value* to be effective. It may take some deep reflection and insight to truly ascertain the spiritual outcome that will best assist a person. For example, do not pray that someone will come into material prosperity. There is no spiritual component to a prayer for that outcome, though it may make someone happy and remove his or her burdens. What is meant by praying for a spiritual outcome is that it should be grounded in spiritual values – outcomes that produce the spiritual fruits of kindness, tolerance, patience, mercy, forgiveness, honesty, strength, courage, and other such noble character traits. These are the real treasures. This is what contributes most to your well-being and happiness. Asking for outcomes other than ones having spiritual value will not come to fruition and may lead to great frustration. You may think that God has forgotten you because your prayer was not answered. This is not true. The prayer was not answered at that time because it did not contribute to someone's spiritual development or their highest good, or the individual may not have been ready to accept the answer.

> Praying for a specific outcome allows certain celestial agencies to cultivate conditions in the mind of the individual or to create a situation that leads a person to ascertain the answers.

The Significance of Prayer

You are not alone. You have angels who watch over you, who are charged to help you grow in spiritual enlightenment and in comprehension of universal reality. You are responsible for your own spiritual growth, and you have been given free will to choose the amount of spiritual growth you desire to achieve during your short life in physical reality. Your free-will choices condition how receptive you will be to accept the changes that can be brought about by effective prayer. No prayer is answered prematurely. God answers all true prayers in time when the person is ready to embrace a new understanding. Perhaps someone is not ready to accept the prayer, or the person's level of development has not yet grown to the point where the petition would achieve its highest good.

It is imperative that your mind be open to the insight and understanding that must precede the change in attitude and behavior. Thoughts reflective of the positive way to act must be clarified before prayer can be answered. It is important to remember that the celestials consider human will when instilling a prayer onto the mind. While much can be done to bring about certain conditions through which a spiritual perspective might be glimpsed, the individual's readiness to accept the changes accompanying the prayer is awaited.

Begin to envision your life as part of a great spiritual adventure – in discovering the universe. The challenges you face in this quest are the opportunities to find the great treasures and beauty of what it means to live in the universe of our Creator's making. Your decisions steer you in certain directions. Your inner spirit guides you to many rewards, upholding and redirecting you along the long road to perfection. Your challenges will be made easier to bear when you are sustained with strength, courage, faith, and hope on the difficult trails.

Your brothers and sisters also face this same great challenge and adventure. Illuminate their path when they are blinded by darkness, when they are lost in despair. Let God's love magnify your light, to help them on their path. Your prayers for them help them find the flicker of light that is their beacon to steer them to our Creator. While you cannot take away their difficulties – their challenges may still exist – God's loving arms are there to uplift and sustain them during their travails.

Prayer is your weapon to fight the evil other people face in their life. If you truly understood the power of prayer, you would more readily use it to overcome difficult situations. Do not think that because you cannot see the results you expect, the prayer has not been heard or answered. A person's difficulties will not be miraculously taken away; the universe does not function this way.

Prayer is most effective when an individual is ready to accept truth, and only the person's indwelling spirit knows when he or she will be most receptive. You must trust the inner spirit to know the best manner and time to help its subject awaken to truth. However, if you want to pray for someone but are unsure what to say, ask that the person be more receptive to their spirit's guidance or more open to God's love. Ultimately this is the goal of prayer – to enlighten others to the truth, beauty, and goodness of our Creator, the love living inside of them.

Your prayers are songs to the celestial beings. On such a troubled world, it is actually music to their ears to hear the petitions for the elimination of poverty, hunger, sickness, hatred, bigotry, anger, greed. In prayer, you act out of love, out of your desire to do good for your brothers and sisters and for your world. And this is how universe operates. Positive intention is the driving force. Love is the currency. Service to others is the product. Serving others through prayer is one way you can assist bringing many into the family of God. It is the means to bring about heaven on earth.

When praying for the eradication of the evil in the world, you literally give the spiritual agencies on this planet the green light to evoke changes in the world's conditions. They accomplish this through a person's conscious willingness to correct their ungodlike actions and find the better way to live. The ideals of spiritual living become impressed upon the human mind, and this recognition inspires the individual to pursue the spiritlike way of living. This is the process of transformation. When enough individuals are transformed, their collective fruits change the culture and yield the noble, civilized society that transcends humanity's animal origins.

You have so much assistance to nurture and uphold you: Your indwelling spirit and innumerable spiritual helpers are poised and ready to offer their guidance and help. Spiritual aid is always there. *Ask for it*. Help for yourself is given when you communicate with our Creator through your inner spirit during stillness. Help for others is offered through prayer. Nothing of real value is ever given without asking. Spiritual gifts are not given to the unappreciative or the unwanting. If you do not choose these things, how can you appreciate and value what you will receive? No person's will is ever superseded. This is true for the society, which represents a collective will, as well as for the individual.

So, be prayerful. Ask for others to pray for you, to help you deepen your understanding and insight into your life's situations, to grow in the love of God. Likewise, help them experience greater self-love and understanding. Seek their edification through prayer. You will continue to develop a deeper concern for their welfare. Your love for others deepens significantly through your sincere and effective efforts to help them gain greater insight into their own spiritual development. Many times, this is the best and only way you can truly help them, especially when they may not be receptive to your words.

If you desire happiness, self-fulfillment, peace of mind and love, then cultivate these spiritual attitudes and habits on a daily basis: stillness and communion with our Creator, real dependence on God, forgiveness, seeing the presence of God in others, service, and prayer. Incorporating these things into your life is the surest way to understand the mysteries of life, the answers to your greatest questions. The purpose of these practices is twofold: to grow in a loving personal relationship with our Creator, and to grow in your understanding of how God expresses His love throughout the universe in the lives of His children. This is the key to spiritual growth. This is the key to life itself.

Serving others through prayer is one way you can assist bringing many into the family of God. It is the means to bring about heaven on earth.

Section III

THE FAITH ADVENTURE

Once you have proclaimed your desire and intention to grow spiritually, your faith becomes activated. This is the dynamic force propelling you toward God. Your inner spirit pilots the living faith that you yield on your adventure of learning about the Creator and the universe. Living in faith is an eternity journey – it is the conscious participation and choice consecration to live according to God's plans. As you progress on this faith adventure, you are guided to those experiences and people who inspire and support your path. And as you grow more confident living in faith, you find that steadfast anchor in the midst of life's chaos, which deepens your love, awe, reverence, and respect for our Spirit Father/Mother's nature and scope of the universe.

13

Faith and the Inner Religious Experience

Dedication to living the eternal values of spiritual reality is living in faith; it is the basis of personal religious experience. It is living that is inspired by an ***inner sense of knowing*** that which is true, that which is real, and that which needs no validation from external sources. Faith is experienced deeply inside the core of your being and is nourished by the living waters of the love of God. The gift of faith has a divine, perfect, and infinite source. Your faith will never lead you astray, but you need to learn how to attune to the voice of your spirit commending you to trust God's love and guidance.

The Nature of Faith

Within your mind is a keen, innate sensing mechanism, a way of knowing internally what is right and true. For many different reasons, this inner sense is often undeveloped. A person may not acknowledge its existence at all or it may be discounted in favor of other abilities, such as reasoning or logic. This inner sensing mechanism is one of the gifts given by the Creator to His children to use as the barometer of the changing course of human and social evolution. It is a steadfast indicator of those eternal and existential values of spiritual reality – what is true, beautiful, and good – that are ceaseless, changeless, and have the ring of authenticity regardless of how far time marches on and how much civilization changes.

How do you know that something is true? How do you assess whether something is real? How do you weigh the value of something? Most people tailor and validate their personal beliefs based on the existing standards of their society. These standards, which range from a personal code of conduct to functioning laws and institutions act as the determinants of acceptable ideas and behavior. Standards evolve from traditions or are set by those individuals whose collective thinking influences the values, mores, and belief systems of institutions or current philosophies or theologies. They condition thoughts, mold decisions, and shape the culture.

But concepts are like people – they evolve over time, down through the generations and centuries. And, just as people have a destiny to increasingly become more godlike as they move from being a material creature to a spirit being, so do concepts evolve from the limitations of human thought toward reflecting the higher ideals of divine reality. Societies move from being primitive and barbaric to civilized and altruistic. If you look at life from a purely material standpoint, then you will constantly assess and validate your experiences at that level; you will see only that which is tangible. However, when you view reality from a spiritual perspective, you begin to sense that there is more than meets the eye. In your attempts to perceive the nature of reality, you will begin to see God in operation; this shift is the catalyst for faith.

You have a superlative mechanism for sensing what is true and real, yet this wonderful gift lies dormant within you. In addition, this world is filled with so much that is negative, that it can be easy to lose sight of those progressively true, beautiful, and good changes that foster real cultural growth. But if you were to take the leap of faith that can lead you into the realm of spiritual living, you would begin to taste the love, joy, and peace that are your foundation and protection against the detrimental aspects of living on this world. Remember, you are a child of a loving Divine Parent!

If it is difficult for you to understand how faith works in human life, consider how a young child grows to trust his or her devoted parents. In a healthy family, the parents love the child; the child feels their love and naturally trusts that they will be really there to provide support, sustenance, and comfort. As this trust grows, so does the certainty that their love and understanding is always available. This is the nature of faith – it is built upon trust. If the child does not feel the parents' love, how can trust grow? And when there is no trust, how can the environment nurture and build faith? The same dynamic of building faith through trust needs to be applied in order for you to grow spiritually and develop your loving relationship with God. Your inner spirit guides you in this relationship with God; however, it is up to you to open yourself to it. Until then, your indwelling spirit is not able to communicate with you in the way it desires, and you may not fully feel the love and comfort your spirit wishes to bestow. Our Creator truly loves you. Your spirit is waiting to enfold you in the divine embrace.

> This inner sensing mechanism in your mind is different from reason and logic. It is a steadfast indicator of those eternal and existential values of spiritual reality – what is true, beautiful, and good – that are ceaseless and changeless, and have the ring of authenticity regardless of how far time marches on and how much civilization changes.

Growing Your Faith

Because you are endowed with free will, it always is your choice whether to seek God or not. Our Universal Father/Mother will never coerce you to love Him or to seek this relationship. But because God is a loving parent, Spirit wants to have a relationship with you. And your indwelling spirit tries to communicate this fact to you through various means. By disclosing the need for a higher power in your life to guide and uphold you, an inner sensing compels you at a certain point to seek communion with God. This is your faith signal urging you to seek God's love via both the intellect and the intuition – and of course, your heart. Then, armed with recognition that you are a beloved child of a benevolent Creator, you become immersed in the dynamic process of growing your faith and harvesting love.

Your developing relationship with God, then, allows for faith to open the door to your indwelling spirit's communication of Spirit's love for you. You gain confidence that God will always be by your side, uplifting you – this is the nature of trust. The more love you feel from God, the greater you will trust in this divine love. The greater your trust, the more your faith blooms to propel you to enjoy deeper levels of God's love and the desire to share your love with God. It is an ever-expanding circle: Faith-love-trust always grows proportionally with your willingness to develop a deeper relationship with God.

> By disclosing the need for a higher power in your life to guide and uphold you, an inner sensing compels you at a certain point to seek communion with God.

Barriers to Faith

Much of the time, your faith lies asleep. You face many stumbling blocks to understanding the true nature of faith. Often a combination of factors creates barriers in your attempts to access your faith. A primary reason may be that your culture is by and large not conducive to spiritual growth. When a society does not place a high value on growing spiritually, the gap between spiritual and material realities widens. When value systems are rooted in tangible rewards, the higher ideals of spiritual living take a back seat. Pursuing material goals above spiritual attainment creates an imbalance both in the individual and in the society.

The great distortion of valuing material acquisition over spiritual attainment places emphasis on acquiring possessions to make your life easier – creature comforts that can build a wall of complacency and isolation by their inherent self-serving nature. Spiritual reality cannot be perceived by eyes that view their own comfort and pleasure as the sole purpose of life. As a culture increasingly embraces this mindset, the reverberations of selfishness produce greed, envy, injustice, and intolerance. These afflictions will reach crisis proportions when left unchecked by spiritual principles that foster *self-control, self-restraint, and self-responsibility*.

Spiritual reality is built upon principles that the changeless, wise, and loving Creator has patterned for the functioning of reality. These principles are forever true. The most fundamental are: *Love is the driving force of the universe. Love is the desire to do good for others*. Love is expressed in relationships – its purpose and intent is the concern for others. The feelings and yearnings produced by love encourage people to weigh their own happiness and comfort against the happiness and the well-being of family, friends, neighbors, community, and the larger society.

Service is love in action. The desire to serve others offsets the self-centered desire for happiness by the recognition of others as equally deserving and worthy of love. There is nothing wrong with desiring happiness for yourself, but if your own happiness is your only concern, this is in violation of the fundamental spiritual principle: Love God; love and serve others. Selfishness (that is, an absence of concern for others) culminates in a lack of self-control. Excessive self-liberty, left unchecked by the guiding force and value of love, inspires havoc of epidemic proportions by its unquenchable thirst for more freedom regardless of the consequences. Unregulated behavior breeds chaos and can create social changes that shake society's foundations to the core.

Loyalty to the principles and values of society's institutions bonds the citizens to these institutions and thus stabilizes civilization. But societal institutions are only successful in maintaining human civilization when people feel supported and uplifted by fundamental values on which they are built. When such institutions are not rooted in values based upon the divine values God has established for the functioning of the universe, they are eventually doomed to failure. Without the higher ideals that foster and stimulate individual growth and cultural development, societal values are simply human creations based upon the narrow perceptions and current interpretations.

Placing your full trust in institutions built upon the limited conceptions of people who do not understand the higher laws of universe order and function is the greatest stumbling block to faith. When these institutions fail, your trust wanes and faith is lost. You do not know where to turn for answers. Society has failed you. But if you were to build your foundation upon spiritual principles – the fact that God loves and supports you at all times – then you would find the strength and peace you seek. Only our Creator is in perfect divine control of the universe. Only God can give you the support and insight you need to make sense out of the problems and chaos of life. Only our Universal Father/Mother can help you sort through the inconsistencies and difficulties you experience and see the divine purpose behind the disarray. Societies and institutions may fail you, but never our Spiritual Parent. You are a beloved child. You have only to call out to God, and Spirit will be there to nurture and guide you. But first, have faith that God's love is there.

If you doubt that God exists and is there for you, then how can Spirit's guidance be revealed? Doubt is a spirit poison blocking the flow of your Divine Parent's communication to you. Doubt is directly related to your unwillingness or inability to believe in a loving, benevolent higher power. A negative concept of God can foster doubts. If this is your experience or idea of God, it will skew your ability to trust. But many people simply don't know and would sincerely like to have some direct confirmation. So, if you doubt in a Divine Universal Father/Mother, ask your spirit if God is real. Tell your spirit you are not sure who God is. Wait for your answer. Faith does not mean coercing yourself to believe in something that you have honest doubts about. But it serves as the catalyst to let your spirit communicate the truth about God to you. When you experience this, *faith is the assurance of inner knowing.*

If you ask with openness and sincerity, you will be released from your doubts about our Universal Father and

Mother. You will arise from your slumber in spiritual darkness and bask in the light of our Creator's love. No human institution will ever give you better insight and understanding or guide you more dependably to overcoming your problems than your loving Spiritual Parent.

> If you were to build your foundation upon spiritual institutions – the fact that God loves and supports you at all times – then you would find the strength and peace you seek.

Living in Faith

Faith is active, living, dynamic. It is revealed in your decisions and actions. It inspires you to live according to the higher ideals of spiritual reality. It compels you to seek truth, inspires you to appreciate beauty, and motivates you to be good. Faith transforms the commonplace into the sublime by elevating your basic human nature to spiritual status through your relationship with divinity. You are not just a child of this world – you are a child of the universe, and as such you have an eternal purpose and goal! Faith replaces your hope for a better future with the assurance of a glorious destiny that awaits you.

Faith is that inner sensing which comes from *the validation of personal experience or from sensing that an idea or ideal is right.* Faith helps you to sense – to intuit – whether something you have just seen or heard is good or true. This is your spirit presence at work, communicating what God wishes you to know. Faith inspires the individual to turn inward for validation. It fills you with peace, contentment, and the assurance of truth, for the validity of the answers received through your faith is not grounded in the external culture or the changing ideas of the human intellect. Faith comes from your inner divine influences, which act as the eternal compass propelling you to your destination in God. Faith illuminates your path through the dark mazes of material existence to glimpse the glory of divine guidance at hand.

When you feel God's love flow through you and you feel good about yourself, you forge a bond with our Divine Creator. You feel a trust connection that increases your capacity to know that your Father/Mother will never forsake you. This is the connecting link with your indwelling spirit. Seeking the stillness allows your spirit to communicate God's feelings for you. Feeling Spirit's love is paramount to increasing your faith, and your faith will expand your capacity to return love to your Spiritual Parent. Allowing your spirit to give you the peace, love, comfort, and compassion God feels for you cements the intangible fact of Spirit's presence.

Because you cannot verify the experience of sensing the presence of God within via the five physical senses, this knowing can only be explained as a matter of faith. Yet somehow you know this experience is real – it is a part of you. Therefore, to augment the faith that will guide your life along spiritual lines of thinking and living, allow yourself to feel God's love and commit yourself to this developing relationship. Faith is like a muscle. You must exercise it in order for it to grow stronger. When it is strengthened, you will radiate the value and purpose of your being. This is the validation of the reality of the experience.

Spiritual reality is good, beautiful, and true, and makes a sensing impression within your being – sometimes going right to the core. When this is registered, you feel loved, peaceful, and happy. These words cannot truly express the depth or breadth that God's love makes you feel, but once you experience it, you know its authenticity, for it is confirmed by the inner ring of truth.

> You are not just a child of this world – you are a child of the universe, and as such you have an eternal purpose and goal! Faith replaces your hope for a better future with the assurance of a glorious destiny that awaits you.

Discerning Faith from Belief

But how do you validate what is real? How can you be sure what to believe? In exploring these questions, it is important to distinguish between faith and belief. A belief may be based on knowledge of facts or a system of ideas that is agreed upon by a large segment of the population. These may or may not be validated by individual experience. Beliefs exist merely at the intellectual level. On the other hand, although faith can have an intellectual component, it transcends belief. Faith can seem reasonable and logical to you, but it is also something more – it is the inner way versus the outer way of knowing.

Seeking validation from external sources to confirm your experiences or beliefs creates the potential for error because a given belief system may or may not have any basis in truth. If the answer does not seem right to you, you may become confused. You are conditioned to listen to the external sources; part of your upbringing is to accept the opinions and beliefs of those who have been educated in a particular subject or in the interpretation of certain theories or theologies. However, their discernment of facts and interpretations of theories may be based on limited perspectives. If the answer reflects only the vantage point of material reality, then an important dimension of the answer is omitted.

You may find yourself struggling between society's stance on a particular belief and a subtle internal signal telling you that something does not feel right about it. To which signal do you listen? Ask yourself, "From what basis are these individuals pronouncing their truth? Is it rooted in love, truth, beauty, and goodness? Does it reflect spiritual values and principles? Does this "truth" yield love, patience, kindness, tolerance, understanding, and compassion? Does it help me feel closer to God? Does it make me more desirous of a relationship with Spirit? Does it produce a greater sense of well-being from a physical, mental, and spiritual standpoint? Does it make me love my brothers and sisters more? Am I more motivated to serve others?" If you ask your inner spirit these questions and the human pronouncement of truth that you are trying to validate does not produce these kinds of fruits, would it be wise to think they were correct?

The spirit living within you has the correct answer. It will never misinform you. Your spirit knows all – it truly is the perfect source of wisdom and goodness. And faith inspires you to attune yourself to that voice of truth. Within each answer, your spirit fragment is declaring to you the more Godlike approach. As your trust in spirit guidance increases, your faith is confirmed in the reflection of godliness. Supported by your faith, your behavior discloses that you are sharing God's love in your daily life. You move from being influenced by the outer environment to loyalty to the inner environment. This is the beginning of the inner religious life.

> Does their "truth" yield love, patience, kindness, tolerance, understanding, and compassion? Does it help me feel closer to God? Does it make me more desirous of a relationship with Spirit?

Personal Religion

Faith is the foundation of religious experience. You may have an intellectual belief in a set of ideas, in dogma, or in a theology; but *faith leads you to act upon your inner knowing of the true way to live.* When you substitute belief for faith, you fall back on relying on another's interpretation instead of using your own perfect inner pilot. At its ultimate level, truth is changeless, for it is divine and perfect – its source is God. However, truth at the human level is relative to your level of ability to comprehend and accept greater and more meaningful facets of universal reality. Cooperating with your indwelling spirit in accepting the insights it wishes to impart conditions your receptivity to truth. Essentially, this is the struggle between your animal and spiritual natures.

Allowing others to dictate what is true substitutes their truth for your truth. This will cause great confusion. While you can certainly listen to another person's perspectives and opinions, attuning yourself to your spirit's guidance will ultimately afford you the best answer. Gradually, you shift from seeing God as something outside of yourself to recognizing the inner relationship you share. This unlocks the door to receiving all that Spirit wishes to share with you – love patience, kindness, compassion, forgiveness, and so on.

These fruits of the spirit are the natural endowments of a life motivated by living faith and inspired by love. When these color your life, your willingness to share these fruits with your brothers and sisters will be alive in your heart. When love and trust open the door, faith steps through and leads you on the road to greater spiritual fulfillment. This is the hallmark of religious living. This is what will transform the world.

The true inner religious life upsteps external belief systems of institutional religions by its influence to transform you into a love-filled, beautiful, and good person. And the fragrance of a person who manifests these qualities is truly inspiring to one's brothers and sisters. They will desire to feel the love you experience; they will want to seek what you have. Regardless of how many or how few are motivated by your example, the internal validation of living a religious life dedicated to spiritual ideals strengthens and sustains in the face of all of life's difficulties. It gives you the courage, insight, and fortitude you need to face those struggles that develop a healthy character.

The Creator's protecting and abiding love, combined with your faith, will be your shield that forever protects you from the harsh realities of material life. *Even though you may still face difficult life circumstances, one day, you will experience the perfection of spiritual reality.* The hope for a better future has great sustaining power. Through the eyes of faith, you can glimpse the reality of the spiritual dimension and the truth that in time all will be made right. What does it matter to the son or daughter of faith if all things earthly crumble? This is the true testament of religious living: steadfastness in God no matter what the circumstances.

Building your relationship with God through faith is the surest inducement to greater self-love, happiness, health, and wisdom. It is the best way to build a noble character that can withstand the painful and perplexing difficulties of life and maintain a dedication to serving others. What can motivate you to become such a person? Taking as your example an individual who dedicated his or her life to these spiritual ideals.

There is a person who lived this faith, who demonstrated unsurpassed love in action. This person dedicated his life to being the supreme inspiration for experiencing God's love and sharing it with others. He lived a perfected human life, dedicated to doing God's will, accepting and enduring all of the vicissitudes of the human condition without protest, anger, resentment, or condemnation. This person is Jesus. He lived on this world, extending love, forgiveness, mercy, tenderness, and understanding to all. Jesus is the inspiration to follow – He is the Way, the Truth, and the Life.

The true inner religious life upsteps external belief systems of institutional religions by its influence to transform you into a love-filled, beautiful, and good person.

13

Jesus, the Living Link

"For God so loved the world, He gave His only begotten Son, that whosoever believed in Him would not perish but have eternal life." Our Divine Creator's gift of Jesus to humanity was and continues to be our inspiration to find true happiness and fulfillment. The Creator never creates intelligent life without providing the proper assistance needed to achieve the highest purpose for which it was created. The purpose of human life is to accept your right, privilege, and responsibility as a child of God through learning, living, and loving. The Spirit Parent's indwelling spirit fragment is your personal guide for leading you to the comprehension of these truths. God, in perfect wisdom, understands that people do not fully use or comprehend the existing relationship between the individual and the spirit guide. Therefore, one of the Creator's children has been designed to play a dual role, acting as the living link between divinity and humanity. This unique child of God has a twofold purpose in living a life on Earth: to lead humans into a loving relationship with our Universal Father/Mother and to disclose the love God has for each child. These purposes are revealed in the life of Jesus.

The Human Jesus

In Jesus lives the inspiration to reach a perfectly balanced state of being on all levels. Jesus achieved the balance between the evolutionary animal nature and the potentials of perfection contained within the inner spirit. Prior to comprehending his divinity status, Jesus was required to live a normal human life and to perfect the potentials of mental, emotional, and human spiritual development. He achieved this by consecrating his decisions and thoughts to seeing every situation, problem, and relationship — all aspects of life — through God's eyes and acting in the way God guided him. In essence, this is doing God's will. In the same manner as you, Jesus had to make decisions and adjustments in his life that fostered his spiritual development. Jesus achieved this to the maximum of human development potential; he attained this perfected state of being as a human. One of his primary objectives in living on this world was to pave the way for all individuals, all evolving children of God, to attain this balanced and noble state of being.

Jesus was a unique personality. It was his human responsibility to master life on this world. It was his divine responsibility to reveal the Universal Father/Mother to His children. No other person could, before or since, claim such duality of identity. In living the mortal life, Jesus essentially faced the same problems you experience. He had a family — a mother, father, sisters, and brothers. Within the existing religious, cultural, and social structure, he had to earn a living to support his family. He experienced every human emotion, feeling, and challenge to faith you do. The decisions he faced in life were similar to yours: what type of work to perform, what kind of relationships to have, how to find self-fulfillment and realization.

Like you, Jesus had an indwelling spirit. Jesus was so receptive to the leadings of his inner spirit that early in life he began to develop his personal relationship with God. As he transitioned from a young child to adolescent to young man, Jesus always turned to his indwelling spirit for guidance and insight in order to meet the challenges and struggles he faced. Similar challenges confront each person — knowing who you are, how to get along with others, discerning your life purpose, navigating the path to fulfillment. Jesus was able to successfully overcome these challenges because of his relationship with God. He recognized our Creator as his Spiritual Parent. He cultivated the love of God within. Unfailingly, he brought everything to the Universal Father/Mother in worshipful communion – in the stillness – which gave him the insight, wisdom, and strength he needed to tackle the problems of living as a human.

> In the same manner as you, Jesus had to make decisions and adjustments in his life that fostered his spiritual development. Jesus achieved this to the maximum of human development potential.

The Significance of Jesus' Human Life

Jesus' inspiration to humanity lies in the truth that he continually turned to his indwelling spirit to adapt his understanding of the problems of daily life to the correct spiritual and divine perspective. His wholehearted devotion to seeking God's guidance in all he did, attuning to the spiritual response, and then following the leadings of his spirit was the single factor in his success in attaining a complete harmonization of human personality and spiritual identity. Jesus mastered this in a relatively short time. When he did achieve this perfected state of being and consecration to God's will as a human, then the fullness of his divinity and his divine purpose were revealed to him.

It was through the cultivation of daily spiritual habits that Jesus was able to achieve this maximization of human potential. He did this by dedicating his life to developing his personal relationship with God. He practiced, developed, and mastered the many spiritual faith-building habits that yield this: seeking the stillness, dependence upon God, forgiveness, seeing the presence of God in others, and prayer. He spent hours in communion with our Universal Father/Mother, seeking guidance and wisdom. The fruit of this endeavor can be gleaned by observing how Jesus treated others with love, understanding, compassion, and mercy. He was able to do this to perfection by consecrating his decision to doing things God's way: loving God, loving and serving humanity. This way to awaken to your true identity and realize your human potential is open to you.

People called him Master as a tribute because they saw in him a mastery of those character traits which so nobly express human life: honesty, courage, understanding, unconditional love, mercy, patience, tolerance, tenderness, wisdom, kindness, and many other fruits of the spirit. His enormous capacity to love was founded on his love for God and of God's love for him. His tremendous capacity to forgive was exemplified in forgiving his enemies, even when he hung dying on the cross. When you ask how you can forgive those who wrong you, picture Jesus on the cross asking our Creator to forgive those who crucified him. This is the very acme of forgiveness. When you want to know how you can see the presence of God in others, **look to Jesus to see how he loved all people** (regardless of their race or religious traditions) because he viewed them as children of our Father/Mother.

Jesus' inner religious life is the inspiration for you to achieve a harmonious synthesis of body, mind, and spirit. When you desire to be guided by God in all your decisions and actions, when you reach the pinnacle of allowing God's ways to be your will, you will achieve an unsurpassed feeling of Spirit's love and a more complete realization of who you are. Knowing how Jesus accomplished this as a human is the greatest understanding of all human knowledge.

Jesus' ability to adapt his thinking toward the enlightened understanding God offered him allowed him to surmount the personal disappointments that are such a large part of human existence. He was able to turn his disappointments into hope and the willingness to trust God in all things. And while your purpose in life may not be the same as Jesus', this dynamic applies to your life. You can choose whether or not to be guided by God. This is the greatest truth of Jesus' human life — his total dedication to seeking God's will.

His mastery of spiritual communion with God afforded him a continuous flow of divine love. Jesus emanated love from every fiber of his being because he was secure in the knowledge that he was a beloved child of God; his very essence was love-saturated. Likewise, your daily practice of seeking the stillness and cultivating the other spiritual habits will lead you to greater self-love and love for others. These are experiences you and Jesus can share.

Jesus' human experience was one component of his revelation of God. In order to depict an expanded portrayal of the loving, merciful, and compassionate nature of our Creator, it was imperative that he appear within a religious tradition that had some understanding of God as a singular personal divine being. This foundation was crucial to Jesus' depiction of God as a loving spiritual parent. However, as part of his divine mission, he cast aside religious and racial barriers to reveal the inclusive nature of Divinity. *This was a revelation of truth that could touch all people because of its appeal to the personal relationship each child shares with his or her loving Divine Parent.*

> People called him Master as a tribute because they saw in him a mastery of those character traits which so nobly express human life: honesty, courage, understanding, unconditional love, mercy, patience, tolerance, tenderness, wisdom, kindness, and many other fruits of the spirit.

Jesus' Divine Mission

Jesus brought people closer to God and God closer to people by serving as the link between humanity and divinity. He showed, by his example of turning inward and seeking the divine presence, how humanity can become perfected, how they can become Godlike. Through the revelation of our Creator's love for each person, Jesus' divine objective was achieved.

In Jesus now lives the embodiment of our Divine Father/Mother. His ministry to others revealed the loving and forgiving nature of the Universal Father/Mother to His children. Seeing Spirit in human form helps people to relate to God as a person. Thus, Jesus is the personal representation of God's love to His human children.

Jesus freely enjoined everyone to enter into the family of God. Through his loving service, he welcomed all people into the universal family. He continually sought the downtrodden, the sick, the troubled in mind, the broken-hearted, and offered a better way of living through the extension of the love and forgiveness God gives to each person. Boundaries of race, religion, culture, and nations are made by humanity; Jesus created no boundaries. No one was ever turned away, regardless of how great the error, or what their religious or racial background was. He extended love, kindness, patience, mercy, compassion, and forgiveness to all seeking salvation and refuge. Indeed, God loves each and every individual in this manner.

Because Jesus exuded such great love, people were attracted to him. They felt the magnetism of his commanding presence. The power of love is a mighty force – it binds people together. The salvation of Jesus' message is: *You are loved regardless of who you are.* This very comforting truth brought hope to the spiritually starved masses. This same message continues today to uplift and heal those in great need.

Jesus knew what people needed in order to rise above their despair, and he freely gave it to all who sincerely and trustingly sought his help. He understood human behavior so well because he had the experience of being human. He could continually accept and love since he comprehended what was and is in the hearts of people. The human component of his dual nature gave him great compassion and empathy for the human condition. He truly could see and understand beyond the actions into the individual's pain and motivation, thereby unlocking hearts and minds to receive God's love, forgiveness, and mercy.

The human component of Jesus' being – his steadfast faith and by his mastery of spiritual communion with Spirit in particular – shows us the way to God. The Divine Jesus reveals the personality and nature of God by his manifestation of our Universal Father/Mother's love and mercy to His children.

Jesus' divinity afforded him the power given to him by God to draw all people to him. The goodness of our Creator was manifested in him. Those who were receptive saw wisdom, understanding, compassion, patience – all the fruits of the spirit alive and free for the asking. His human/divine life is the superior revelation of a Divine Parent who is approachable to all who desire this relationship because of Spirit's tender nature. As Jesus loves, so does our Spiritual Father/Mother. As Jesus forgives, so does God. Look to Jesus to see our Creator's personality. Jesus is the indispensable link between Spirit and humanity. Even now, through Jesus' Spirit of Truth, He invites all people to feel that love – drawing everyone into the spiritual family of God.

> These are the greatest truths taught by Jesus: All people are beloved by God. Everyone is welcome into the family of God. You are a child of a loving and compassionate Spiritual Father/Mother. By faith you receive the gift of sonship.

Jesus' Inspiration for Human Life

"The Kingdom of Heaven is within." This pronouncement of the truth of your indwelling spirit that links you to God is the foundation of spiritual development. Stillness, communion with Spirit, is your path to that kingdom. Jesus bestowed great enlightenment upon all people with this pronouncement, which continues to challenge those individuals of faith to seek the inner life. The love of God lives in you. It is your choice whether to seek this innate love. Following the inspiration of Jesus' life, adapting your habits to commune with your Creator, forgiving, praying, and seeing the presence of God in others will lead you to the sublime satisfaction of living in the divine family. The beauty and symmetry of Jesus' personality lie in his mastery of these four practices. He was the master artisan who crafted a polished and noble character out of a raw human nature. This is the way to mold your character into a true work of art, into an object of great beauty.

Jesus revealed himself as the Son of Man. He lived naturally just as you must; he employed no superhuman powers to meet the challenges of his material living. His unsurpassed faith in God's loving guidance led him to triumph over the obstacles he faced through life. He represented all of humanity to our Universal Father/Mother in his portrayal of the Son of Man as he disclosed the true path of finding God. He presented to our Divine Creator how humanity could reach a perfected state of being – the freewill mind totally attuned to the divine will. Jesus shares this way to all seekers of truth. He is every human's inspiration to find divinity.

Jesus' lessons, or parables contain many meanings and depictions of the nature, personality, and love of God and how our Creator seeks companionship with His children. They also reveal many examples of how to treat your brothers and sisters in a Godlike manner. You have been given an inner sensing mechanism to recognize the truth of the meanings of these parables. But parables are but one means of Jesus' depiction of truth. His greatest gift is in the life he led to inspire you to act upon the truths he taught.

His credo of the kingdom of heaven within was proclaimed to all so they would seek the inner life. This message cut through the need for appealing to priests or other theologians to interpret Deity. Jesus demonstrated the way to develop a direct personal relationship with God. During his public ministry, he upset the ecclesiastical structure of the Jewish religion by his exhortations to develop a personalized religious code of living instead of relying on rituals and dogma as the means to gain salvation.

Jesus' death on the cross was the natural repercussion of fear-ridden actions by a threatened power structure in danger of losing its authority. It was not necessary for him to die in that manner to redeem people! *God was not demanding vengeance in the form of the death of His innocent Divine Son for the collective sins of humanity.* What loving parent would want his or her child to be punished for the errors committed by someone else or by a collective group of young children? The depiction of an angry, vengeful Supreme Being does not conform with Jesus' revelation of God as a loving, tender, merciful, and compassionate Creator and Universal Father/Mother. Unfortunately, the concept of sacrifice as the means of salvation was an embedded tradition in the culture of many peoples in Jesus' day. Consequently, it became assimilated into the theology of the Christian teachings that developed after his resurrection.

God does not desire or require His children be punished for their errors, nor does He extort a sacrifice for their salvation. Humans punish themselves by cutting themselves off from God's love when they do not follow the divine way placed before them. Our Creator's love always surrounds you, but you might not choose to seek this. You may feel tainted by sin, but those feelings or thoughts separate you from your Divine Parent only in your own mind and heart. In actuality, we are never separated from God.

Nevertheless, there is great meaning in the death of Jesus on the cross. Jesus was so totally dedicated to our Universal Father/Mother that he could follow the natural progression of events leading up to his betrayal, humiliation, and horrific death on the cross. This he endured because of his unwavering faith in God, which gave him the strength and comfort to sustain him during this most trying ordeal. Such faith transcends all evil. Such faith is the supreme gift of Jesus to his children. It portrays a far-seeing trust that transcends the shortsighted eagerness to be relieved of your hardships.

God does not arbitrarily step in and deliver you from adversity. Jesus followed the natural course of events to demonstrate to humanity how God grants – through your faith – the courage, strength, insight, and hope to sustain you through the despair of material difficulties. Jesus met his ignominious death with grace, poise, serenity, and forgiveness. He was able to do that because our Creator's love sustained him. God's and Jesus' love and comfort, likewise, are there for you whenever you need them.

Jesus said, "I do not promise to deliver you from the waters of adversity, but I do promise to accompany you through them." He is the supreme inspiration of trust in divine love. No greater example of love has ever been shown than in Jesus' willingness to lay down his life for his children to demonstrate how our Universal Father/Mother is with you always, even in the most horrendous situations.

Jesus' faith sustained him through the experience of death, the experience people all have in common. This was his final objective in revealing to humans how to transcend the material life through faith. For life on Earth is just the first step in an eternal career of approaching our Universal Creator through exploration of the universe. Jesus' resurrection is living proof that life continues after cessation of the energies that animate the physical body. The new body of his resurrection is the vehicle similar to the one you will use as you continue your life once you have transcended the physical earthly career. Take comfort in the truth that life continues after death. Be uplifted to know that there is one divine person who shares with you the human experience, one who truly understands all that you must endure.

Jesus lived and died as a human. He revealed to humanity the way to achieve the perfect balance between the physical, mental, and spiritual levels of living by turning all decisions and aspirations to our Divine Creator. He met life's challenges by looking inward to his indwelling spirit for the answers, by trusting God to guide him. You have this potential if you dare to challenge your faith to claim the love living inside you. But it is through this superhuman power and love that lives inside you that you are inspired to achieve such a heightened state of being.

And now, Jesus' divine status commands full authority over heaven and earth. He sends his ministering spirit to reveal the love of God for his children to all who are ready to listen. This Spirit of Truth is available to you to draw Jesus near whenever you need to feel Christ's presence by your side. Divine sustenance is forever close at hand. Empathy for the human experience is fully accessible in Jesus. The glory of Divinity is fully revealed in Christ. In Jesus, "He who has seen me has seen the Father." He speaks to his children:

"I live in the hearts and minds of all. I am your father and your brother. I am the creator of your universe. We are family and I lived among you as one of you. In all things, look to me for answers. Look to me to see our Father. Seek me in all you do, and the way of happiness and peace will be yours. My Spirit of Truth overshadows you and my love abides in you. I am the comfort of all the ages. I am the living water. I am the bread of life. I am the way."

14

Healing: Becoming a Whole Person

Healing is the gift of your Spiritual Parent. It is bestowed by grace to each child when there is a sincere and faith-filled desire to follow God's ways. While it can be helpful just to understand that you have been designed to live in a state of harmony in accordance with universal law, achieving this state of balance is a lifelong process that gradually unfolds as you become increasingly God-conscious. Healing is the step that corrects what is out of balance to bring it back to a state of grace.

The Divine Plan contains certain laws of functioning for spirit, mind, and matter. And it is Spirit's desire for you to achieve great health and happiness by functioning in accordance with these laws. You are composed of spiritual, mental, and physical matter and energies that have been designed by the highest intelligence and power – your Spiritual Parent. Each component of your being is designed to function in unison with the other two; each must be nourished with the proper fuel if it is to maintain this delicate state of balance between spirit, mind, and matter. Conversely, ignoring one or more elements of God's wholistic plan creates an imbalance that can potentially deteriorate your entire state of being. When diseases of the body, mind, and spirit occur, there are means of correction and restablization to restore good health. And understanding the nature of your spiritual, mental, and physical components will make you a more conscious participant in the ongoing nurturing and development of your well being. But it is actually God who heals.

Spiritual Healing

In seeking healing, it is important to begin at the spiritual level. Here is where your inner spirit can activate positive energy, beginning the chain reaction that will reverberate to your mental and physical levels of being. While most people attempt to heal themselves solely with physical medicines and approaches, true healing occurs at the spiritual level, where God exists. Our Creator, as the source of spirit and energy, sets the wheels of the universe in motion. Then, by downstepping universal energies from the very highest spiritual vibration to the dense vibration of physical matter, Spirit unifies, coordinates, and integrates all the life-producing energies into certain vibratory patterns that impinge upon the three different levels of your reality: spiritual, mindal (mental/emotional), and physical. Therefore, when you attend to the needs of your spirit first, your mind and body begins to rebalance. Thus you maintain peace and harmony – free from the stress that so devitalizes your health.

Communion with God is spiritual nourishment. It is the meeting ground of Divine Source and human child – it is the place where God gives you everything you long for. In stillness, communing with your Spirit Parent banishes those spiritual diseases of abandonment, despair, grief, and resentment. It is not God's wish for you to experience these isolat-

ing feelings: they are human-created. They may be amelio-
rated by human love, but they cannot be eliminated by anything other than God's love. You are powerless to remove
these deeply rooted wounds.

To receive spiritual healing is simply a matter of asking for it; it is automatically bestowed by grace. Yet you may
unconsciously have blocks that impede the full reception of
complete spiritual healing. But God sees what your heart
longs for and wants to grant your request. Your Divine
Father/Mother sees what you cannot. You are a pearl of great
value underneath your pain, shame, and despair. Ask God to
find the valuable treasure that you are and release it from
underneath the layers of painful experiences. Devotedly will
your Spirit cover you with the greatest healing balm in the
universe – unconditional love. With new eyes, you will see
yourself as God sees you. This is the beginning of spiritual
healing, and it is available to everyone, regardless of how
undeserving you may think you are.

Spiritual healing has stillness at its heart; communion with God activates it. Healing continues with each
moment spent in the stillness. This is the time to feed your
soul. Daily spiritual communion significantly diminishes any
disconnection from God you may feel. It augments your
faith to know with increasing assurance that you are a
beloved child of a very compassionate, affectionate, and merciful Spiritual Parent.

Spiritual healing has the dual effect of rejuvenating
the body as well as calming the mind. You are given everything you need in order to live more successfully. Claim
what is rightfully yours!

You are a pearl of great value underneath your pain, shame, and despair. Ask God to find the valuable treasure that you are and release it from the layers of painful experiences

Emotional Healing

Emotional healing harmonizes your self-concept with the dawning awareness of yourself as a child of a loving and Divine Spiritual Parent. The dual effect of knowing and feeling God's love activates your intellect and intuition to stay true to your innate moral nature. Most people have a sense of what is right and wrong – moral responsibility. If this awareness is based on a positive view of yourself as a child of a loving Creator Parent, usually there is harmony between what you know and how you act.

Balance is found in the integration and consistency in between thoughts and actions. Although people can often think noble and laudable thoughts, how many times do they fall short in their actions? Ideally, a moral concept concerning a given situation should sponsor a reaction consistent with that concept. However, when there is tension between the intellect (knowing) and intuition (feeling), you may think you understand a concept while your actions may speak otherwise. You may say that you love humanity, for example, but if you treat others with scorn or intolerance, there is great inconsistency between what you believe and how you act. If harmony existed between what you know and how you feel, you would naturally and spontaneously act accordingly. Emotional healing is the great equalizer of these two aspects.

Good mental health is reflected in the capacity to clearly and rationally reach decisions about your life that will lead you to the greatest sense of self-authentification. In the stillness, you gather the mental energy you need to understand life situations and experiences by partaking in our Creator's wisdom and guidance. You discern with increasing clarity those insights that help you meet your challenges. Decisions once difficult to make will seem to come easier as your trust grows in this divine guidance. Your spirit is diligently striving to help you to triumph over the challenges you face. While you may still need to face challenging circumstances in order to grow, you have greater spiritual and mental tools and strength to cope with the situations you encounter. *Your problems do not suddenly disappear – your ability to handle them improves.*

Consequently, what emerges is an awareness that what you experience in life is just an exploration of learning new ways to master different situations and relationships. In stillness, you have the opportunity to creatively see new truth meanings that liberate you from the paralyzing fear that impedes decision-making and destroys your ability to act effectively. You find the answers to your problems and are given the strength to overcome your difficulties. God's love and wisdom comes with a steady hand that guides your thoughts and influences your actions. Your spirit dissolves your fears in a gentle and supportive way. And as you develop your potential for seeing universal meanings and values, new facets of your personality are expressed in very satisfying ways. Mental activity becomes refreshing, stimulating, and regenerating instead of confusing and exhausting.

Clear mental activity is the foundation of emotional stability. Any negative thinking, past or present, impedes your indwelling spirit's communication. Those hurtful thoughts, experiences, and behaviors hidden deep within the psyche can only be eliminated by the power of Spirit. Whenever you feel that those deeply rooted unlovely behaviors are taking hold of you, this is your signal to return to the inexhaustible divine wellspring of God's love. Call upon the power of Spirit to enter your thoughts and turn them to the spiritual perspective. Summon the presence of God into your body; your Universal Father/Mother will correct that which is hurtful and spiritually align it. As this happens, no judgment is placed upon you for any mistakes you may have made in the past. You may feel dirty or shameful, **but God does not judge you.** What is actually occurring at this level of emotional healing is the simple tension-releasing correction of God. This energy encircuits you with the correct spiritual insights and perspectives that reveal the better way to live. It is a lightness and joyfulness you are now inviting into your being. Anytime you are in the grip of your negative behavior patterns, that is your internal signal to again come to the well. Return to the stillness and let the loving waters of God wash over and purify you. It is a time of great delight!

Everything negative that has happened to you can be corrected through the power of your Universal Father/Mother. **This will happen when you renew yourself in God's love.** Once the corrections are made, then you are free to reconnect with or develop those noble characteristics of courage, patience, kindness, honesty, and tolerance. You will actually become a positive force to battle anger, hatred, and intolerance. You will be upheld by a spirit that no one will be able to diminish, no matter how unjust is their treatment of you.

When so motivated by Spirit, you are forever liberated from those previously enslaving behaviors that society must regulate by fear-inspired rules. When you live in the spirit, you are good naturally. You live freely – life becomes more spontaneous and natural. This is the hallmark of an emotionally responsible and mature individual, one who has awakened to abundant richness of spiritual reality. The emotional life of such an individual is peaceful, happy, purposeful, and immensely satisfying.

> Those thoughts and behaviors hidden deep within the psyche can only be eliminated by the power of Spirit. At those times when you feel those deeply rooted unlovely behaviors have taken hold of you, that is your signal to return to the inexhaustible divine wellspring of God's love.

Physical Healing

Everyone wants to enjoy very good health – freedom from disease, pain, restriction in movement. But over time, habits are developed through improper diet, stress, and lack of exercise that destroy the body's natural processes from working in the way they were intelligently designed by God. In asking for physical healing from your Divine Source, it is helpful to be aware of certain parameters that condition how much healing can occur.

God has the power to correct any illness, genetic defect, or any other physical or emotional impairment as He so desires and wills. It is a mystery quite outside the limits of human understanding reserved by Spirit why healing occurs for some people and not for others. It is not helpful to compare what you experience with what another person experiences. Healing must be approached in faith, with the individual coming to God devoid of anything but the most sincere, childlike trust.

There are those spontaneous corrections of diseases that defy human understanding for the power of Spirit has the capacity to change anything according to God's will. There are times when the more gradual evolution of healing unfolds. As you ask for healing, do not presume which form it will take. Trust, however, that your highest good is God's desire for you and be grateful for whatever kind of healing your Divine Parent offers.

In any case, the physical body responds to the healing power of Spirit by correcting problems according to physical laws God has established for normal physical operations. The loving power your Divine Father/Mother employs in healing you manifests itself in the physical world and fulfills certain universal laws that have been created for the maintenance and control of physical reality and human life. Matter and energy move in specific patterns; your body was designed to work in harmony with those universal plans. Conversely, if energy or matter is distorted in violation of these laws, chaos and disease ensue.

Aligning yourself in the flow of God's love during your stillness practice allows the unity, wholeness, and connection you share with Spirit to your mind to manifest. Your mind, in turn, transforms the positive energy of spirit into those impulses that stimulate your body into certain healing activities. As God heals you, your body's processes return to normal; this reflects the symmetry of the spirit-mind-body connection.

Spirit is information. Mind is the circuit. Body is the receptor. The mind circuit connects into the physical brain, translating the spiritual impulses into mental and emotional images that send electric/biochemical signals to the brain, culminating in cell functioning. Spirit is intelligence and energy springing forth from God. Spirit contains the information about the processes that have been created to generate and maintain life. The body is innately intelligent because it has been programmed by your Divine Source.

Each cell in your physical body has the capacity to receive and be corrected by universal love. What actually corrects cell functioning is a form of light that Spirit infuses within your being. Think of your body as a sponge soaking up every bit of God's healing loving light, for in reality that is what is occurring. This healing love-light is an energetic stimulus for every subatomic, cellular, molecular, tissue, and organ component of the body. This energy is what actually animates the body; and if it were not present, then life would cease to function.

Each living cell within your mechanism vibrates. It resonates at a certain harmonic frequency that has been designed by your Divine Source. When you are out of tune or ill, your body no longer resonates in accordance with its original design. To heal physically, therefore, your body must regain its original and healthful harmonic resonance. This is what the hand of God corrects within you when you avail yourself of Spirit's healing power. Divine action is the most powerful energy in the universe.

In the stillness, as you commune with God, you are actually healing; you are partaking of divine energy. During this time, it is helpful to envision the spiritual hands of your loving Father/Mother in the afflicted areas of your body. Ask for the healing energy to flow into you. Ask for the presence of Spirit to infiltrate those diseased areas. You will sense a stirring deep within. Your cells are being altered.

Our Creator has given us marvelous vehicles in which to live. When your body is supported and nourished on the gifts God has given you to sustain life, health flourishes. Harmony between the spirit, mind, and body is gradually established the more you follow the leadings of your inner spirit as it guides you to achieve the highest state of human existence – balance.

> The physical body responds to the healing power of Spirit by correcting those problems according to physical laws God has established for normal physical operations.

Achieving Balance

Each component of your being – your spirit, mind, and body – must command your attention and be afforded the proper nourishment if you wish to enjoy that exquisite harmony of balance.

God has given you everything you need to sustain life and health on this planet. Your bodies were designed to work in tandem with nature – to co-exist and be supported by nature. However, you have done much to hurt yourselves through the consumption of manmade chemicals. Many of these chemicals, which were not meant to be ingested into the physical mechanism now reside within the cells themselves. People often consume poor quality food, tainted water, and polluted air because of this infiltration of unwarranted chemicals, so the cellular structure of the body has become changed over time. The cells are not as viable. They therefore tend to reject the proper nutrition and repel the energy sparks they need to function normally.

It is imperative that your body be nourished by those substances and energies it needs to keep it strong and healthy. A diet that replenishes the living nutrients your body requires will enhance the flow of energy to improve cellular function. The natural vegetation of this world sustains the well-being of your physical mechanism because its bio-chemical composition and energy have been developed by Spirit to nourish and maintain the body. Daily exercise also contributes to cell viability as it detoxifies, tones, and strengthens the many processes so vital to longevity and flex-ibility.

But the most effective destressing and health-induc-ing nourishment you can offer your body is the practice of stillness. In stillness, you are able to more acutely discern the actual presence of the energy of God's love. This love ener-gy affects all three levels of your being; great therapeutic effects will be felt if you sustain your stillness practice for longer lengths of time. Direct it into your cells, into your organs – let it envelop your entire being. This is a powerful inducement for your body to achieve the balanced harmon-ic frequencies it was designed to hold. The more you focus on God healing you, the greater the healing effect. Devoting part of your stillness time to asking God to reenergize your body will not only improve your health, it will unify all the components of your being into a strong and whole character.

Ask God to heal you each time you are in stillness. In lieu of a spontaneous remission of your symptoms, even serious damage can be corrected over time. You cooperate with the healing process by following a patient, long-range disciplined approach through developing those healthy phys-ical, mental, and spiritual habits required for the body to respond beneficially. If you truly want to enjoy health at these levels, cultivate those daily habits.

There is no shortcut; there is no pill you can take to correct your problems. God will help you overcome your obstacles, but you must first desire it, and then be willing to follow the leadings of your spirit that guide you to resolution. Sometimes this means working with certain limitations of body that cannot be changed. If so, even if you are not healed of your physical ailments, cultivating these habits will lead you to accept your condition with serenity and help you to enjoy life to the fullest. Ultimately, this is the real goal of healing.

A healthy state of being is beautiful. Radiant, glowing energy emanates from a unified, balanced individual. Happiness, serenity, and love exudes from an inspired soul who is living human life at the highest levels. Healing is nothing more than the process of unifying the three aspects of physical, mindal, and spiritual reality into a balanced state of being. Usually, disease and disharmony are directly attributed to one, two, or all three components being in disarray. God unifies all three into a harmonious balance when you are in the stillness. Spirit guides you to find the way to treat your physical body in the proper manner, providing you are receptive to the information you are given. Spirit instills those insights and thoughts that help you master the problems and challenges in your life. Spirit will embrace you and you will feel the deepest love attainable – God's love. Through your inner spirit's revelations, you will be revitalized to fulfill your potential and become the person you know, deep inside, is aching to be expressed.

This is the call of the perfection hunger that God instills in you to propel you toward Spirit. It is what your inner spirit, ultimately, strives to awaken in you to propel you toward the joys and treasures of spiritual living. When you awaken to this realization and live inspired by the lure of perfection attainment, new adventures of enlightenment and opportunities to vibrantly express life are waiting for you, this reborn child of the universe. Will you answer the call and awaken to the glorious future that beckons you?

Devoting part of your stillness time to asking God to reenergize your body will not only improve your health – it will unify all the components of your being into a strong and whole character.

15

Spiritual Growth and the Ascension Career

Spiritual growth would be futile and meaningless unless there was a sense of a future, a destiny, attached to it. Why would a God who lives in perfection create experiential beings if not for them to acquire perfection at some future point? Why would spiritual growth have to be so hard won on the battlefield of struggle and choice if not for the greater reality planned in which experience and knowledge can be put to use? Something much larger than you could ever imagine awaits you if you choose the path of spiritual growth – a destiny to thrill you beyond the depths of your imagination and satisfy you beyond the desires of your dreams.

The Personality and the Soul

You are given the gift of life because of our Creator's love for you. In order to move through life, you must have an identity that sets you apart from others – a way for you to be distinctly identified as "you." *This is your personality and it is bestowed as the most precious gift: your birthright to exist.* You may have considered personality as the character you develop as part of your experiences in conjunction with the traits you inherit – but it is something much more. It is the composite fundamental identity of your personhood that makes you unique.

You gather experiences and gain knowledge as you live. These experiences and insights become housed within your personality as you expand your self-expression. Some experiences, such as eating breakfast or driving a car, happen at the most basic level of material existence and do not have real impact on who you are becoming. But other accumulated experiences, particularly those of being in relationships with people, have deeper meaning – they have spiritual value. The amount of spiritual reality you have come to recognize and experience in the life you lead on this world is your soul.

How much did you come to love God, love yourself, love other people? Were you honest, kind, compassionate, or were you dishonest, insincere, and unforgiving? Did you show tolerance and patience to your fellows, or were you prejudiced and self-righteous? To what extent did you forgive yourself and others? How much did you serve humanity with unselfish love and compassion? These are the actions that reflect spiritual values.

The spiritual truths you were able to recognize and enact in your life exist within your personality, and they survive physical death. Experiences of the material life, on the other hand, do not survive. Your personality plus your spiritual experience combine to make your soul. It is your soul that moves on to the next level of existence. And it is then that you begin another phase of your life as you progress toward fulfillment of the command, "Be you perfect as I am perfect."

> In order to move through life, you must have an identity
> that sets you apart from others – a way for you to be
> distinctly identified as "you." This is your personality
> and it is bestowed as the most precious gift:
> your birthright to exist.

The Choice of Eternal Life

All of life is a journey godward. The extent to which you allow yourself to be led by your inner spirit in order to eradicate your character defects is the measure of how far you have grown in comprehending and living in spiritual truth. This brings you closer to God. At a certain point in your development, you will be given the opportunity to make your final decision about whether to continue on the spiritual path. This may or may not happen on Earth. When that decision is sealed – when it is your will to always choose the divine path – then your spirit and your personality become as one. At this point, your inner spirit is no longer a fragment of God, for humanity and divinity have conjoined to form this new entity, this budding spiritual child ascending toward perfection attainment. This is the beginning of eternal life.

Living on Earth with all its evil, it is difficult to embrace the truth that the universe is truly dominated by love and goodness. You may view this world as a dark canvas and see only occasional points of goodness and truth. However, reality is not at all like this. The universe of God is truly a fabric of love, with dark spots of fear and evil where those exist who do not know God and Spirit's truth, beauty, and goodness. God is obscured from view in those individuals lost in the dark. But truly, no matter how far away God may seem to you, our Universal Father/Mother has never left your side; only your choices have pulled you away.

However, you must be aware there are consequences to the choices you make while still in physical form. How you decide to act on this world determines where you will continue your growth and development on the next. Choosing to grow spiritually, to live in love and goodness, will advance you to a higher level of spiritual education on the next world. On the other hand, if you treat yourself with guilt and self-hatred, and treat others with anger and intolerance, you are turning yourself from God and spiritual reality and you will first need to correct these attitudes on the next world before continuing your ongoing education at higher levels. If you cannot face the consequences of your mistakes on this world, then through God's merciful plan, you are given the opportunity on the next to fully realize the implications of how you chose to live.

Rehabilitation comes in the form of teachers who will lead you step by step, lovingly helping you to rectify the errors you have committed against yourself and others. You come to realize that your unlovely actions were due to a lack of insight into spiritual reality or a failure to embrace spiritual concepts. These teachers gently help you overcome whatever obstacles hampered your ability to embrace spiritual truth.

Loving guidance is the greatest impetus for doing good. This instruction from your guides, who are valiantly trying to help you overcome the actions of the past – along with your heightened capacity to attune yourself to your spirit's guidance – will provide you with a greater opportunity to realize the wonder, beauty, and joy of spiritual living in God's family. At the point when you have become fully awakened to these universal truths, your ultimate decision must be made: whether to continue to exist.

From the enlarged perspective of reality you have attained, you make the supreme decision of whether you wish to continue to live. That is, you must make the ultimate choice of whether to or not to embark upon the path of spiritual enlightenment that paves the way to eternal life. You decide. Every person has this choice to make. Those who continue to embrace error and evil are in effect rejecting the spiritual path, rejecting God – and ultimately, rejecting life. That is, they are making a choice that has as its final consequence the cessation of their own existence. This is because the path of spiritual growth is the way of love – it is the true reality of the universe – whereas evil, as the antithesis of all that is good, beautiful, and true, actually does not exist in the universe of spirit. Continuing to choose anger, hatred, intolerance, and other evils is therefore the equivalent of choosing unreality. At that point of choice, you cease to be, and become as if you never were.

God forgives all error and all wrongdoing. A loving spiritual Creator/Parent does not desire to be separated from His children, nor does the Universal Father/Mother condemn them to eternal suffering. However, when you continue to act in ways not reflective of love, truth, goodness and beauty, you are rejecting the path to perfection God has established. You therefore continue to identify with that which is unreal. When you do not recognize this unreality, how can you learn a better way? How can you develop the insight into the beauty and righteousness of the God-given way? The inability to see things from God's perspective limits your capacity to accept God's offer of love. It prevents you from seeking the eternal life. This is why you are given so much assistance after physical death – to give you the optimal opportunity to choose eternal life rather than extinction.

Physical death is only the passing from one plane of existence to another. It is that simple. There is no reason to fear this transition, for it is the gateway to more love than you have ever experienced. It is the threshold to the adventure of life. The children of God who are dominated by love and who trust in faith know that God has secured their place in the universal family and they look forward to the new life. However, those who fear death – either because they have doubt and uncertainty about the spiritual life or are conscious of the wrongs they have committed – have difficulty making this transition. For them, the anticipation of death brings all doubts and mistakes to the forefront of consciousness and places a heavy burden upon their psyche.

During the transition from the physical life to the spiritual life, your inner spirit is diligently working to smooth the way and help you glimpse the wonder and beauty of the next life. But how can your spirit convey the truth of the eternal life and the love waiting for you when you resist with guilt and doubt? The mystery of death is shrouded only by your lack of insight into the nature of spiritual reality and your relationship with God. Embrace the insights that are trying to be communicated to you and walk forward into the light beckoning to the new life.

> From the enlarged perspective of reality you have attained, you make the supreme decision of whether you wish to continue to live. That is, you must make the ultimate choice of whether to or not to embark upon the path of spiritual enlightenment that pavesthe way to eternal life. You decide.

The Next Life

Living and growing is an experiential and evolving continu-um. When you leave this planet after passing through physi-cal death, and awaken on a new world of spiritual dimension, your evolving soul will be housed in a new body – a new sensing mechanism. This new body is equipped with *enhanced capabilities to discern spiritual truth and adapt to your new environment of spiritual reality.* Upon awakening at this new level of reality, you begin your spiritual career in earnest, for you will be able to see that which was shielded from you in the physical life. And you will pick up your life exactly where you left off on this world.

At first, adapting to a new environment will fill you with wonder and a sense of disbelief, for you will not appre-ciate what has happened to you or understand where you are. But after your initial adjustment, you will remember your identity, the person you were during your existence on Earth. Your growth will continue from this point of your character development. You will continue to learn through progressive experience as you did while in the physical form.

Whatever serious personality defects you had in your physical life will be rehabilitated with the assistance of loving instructors. It is their responsibility to teach the joys of spiritual reality to those who led a spiritually deprived life on the material worlds of their nativity.

As your life unfolds in this new dimension, you will recognize family and friends who have gone before as you; you will reacquaint yourselves with them and share your thrilling experiences with one another. You will see them as you never have before and be able to work out the differences and problems you struggled with on the physical sphere. You will be able to share the kind of relationship you truly desired to have with them, but which could not happen on Earth, for whatever reason.

If grave injustices were committed against or by you on this world, you will have the opportunity to heal these wounds. No longer need you be embittered by anger or pain. The many loving teachers that help you work through these problems guide you patiently and skillfully to grasp the deeper meanings and significance of these experiences. Ultimately, you will reach an understanding of the situation and be able to forgive those who deeply hurt you.

Also, your rehabilitation will guide you to seek forgiveness from those whom you hurt. It will be your responsibility and your privilege at that time to forgive and be forgiven, for you will be filled with compassion and love. Your forgiveness is the measure of your love and understanding. Thus you will want to forgive and be forgiven, for you know in your soul that it is God's way.

> If grave injustices were committed or by you on this world, you will have the opportunity to heal these wounds.

The Eternal Adventure
of Universe Discovery

At some point in your new life, you will discern that spiritual mastery is a very long, progressive accomplishment. Your ascension career is just that – a career, one that will be achieved over eons of time. You will be enrolled in training schools where in-depth instruction and varied tasks will be part of your spiritual education. But life will be challenging and exciting as you strive for spiritual perfection by mastering the assignments that will be presented to you. You will not be sitting idle playing on a harp in the clouds; you will lead a very productive and fulfilling life. Your experiences will consist of finding new ways to express God's love to others and recognizing our Universal Father/Mother in all that surrounds you. This is the true meaning of eternal life.

Your personality will reveal expanded levels of creative expression as you discern new meanings within the universe. Because your identity is an expression of God, the way you express your personality within spiritual meanings and values uncovers a new facet of the immensity and grandeur of the Creator. Comprehending your true identity as you joyfully experience activities that satisfy your personality expression will bring you closer to God as you are flooded by the enormity of Spirit's love for you. It is this love for you that makes the ascension career possible. And if you choose this path, you will forever find deeper and richer ways to fully enjoy life and satisfy your craving for the perfection that brings you closer to our Universal Father/Mother.

As you grow in universe recognition of spiritual reality, you are given increasingly sensitive abilities to feel, intuit, know, smell, taste, and see the beauty surrounding you. Philosophy, music, art, and science of cosmic proportions heighten your awareness of the glories you experience every day, urging you forward in your perfection hunger for greater love, knowledge, and understanding of the Creator and the universal family. You will be given ample opportunity to fully satisfy your desire to do anything you wish – provided it has spiritual value. Life will never be boring or dull again. There is too much to do, too many people to meet, too much love to share for you to become disillusioned or complacent.

Love surrounds you in the presence of countless other celestial beings waiting to help you in whatever way they can. Whenever you have a problem, someone will be there to assist you. No longer will you have anything to fear, nor will you feel alone. These are your brothers and sisters – living expressions of God's love, just as you are. You will be given companions to accompany you and to help you master your lessons of spiritual growth.

But, as with life on Earth, there will be challenges to face; even at the spiritual level of existence, progressive evolutionary creatures must learn and achieve one level at a time. This entails constant decision-making and attuning your choices to God's will. But the love and assistance available to you will touch and inspire you to greater levels of spiritual development.

The joyful truth is that the whole universe is your playground and training ground. In your quest to understand the universe, you will travel to faraway worlds – and you will have an eternity to do this. The spiritual union of you and your conjoined spirit unfailingly urges you toward greater truth and understanding of the realities of God and the universe. And one day, when you have perfected yourself and are ready to meet the Creator face to face, you will finally stand in the presence of the Universal Father/Mother, the One in Whom All Things Exist. You will linger there in the divine spirit presence and tell God of your journey to Paradise, as you luxuriate in divine love and glory. God's precious child has been returned – you are now fully spirit. And you are ready to begin an even more glorious and exciting destiny of universal service!

So begin NOW! Realize who you are! You can start your eternity career today by recognizing the presence of God within you. The sooner you begin, the sooner you will realize and appreciate this glorious destiny that awaits you. You can have heaven on earth if you are willing to develop your relationship with your inner spirit – by seeking the stillness each day, forgiving, depending upon God, and seeing the presence of God in others. All of the joy our Spiritual Parent's love can be had today.

Our Creator Father/Mother is waiting for you. You only have to ask for Spirit's love and it will happen. All of the peace and happiness you could ever desire will be given to you. This is God's promise. Awaken to the greatness living in you.

Section IV

FINALE

16

The Future

These teachings about the nature of spiritual growth have been given as a gift to encourage us to turn to God and develop that deep internal love connection that binds us to a larger universal reality. I sincerely hope these lessons will inspire and encourage us to seek our own enlightenment in an effort to heal this planet. However, it is our choices that determine if we will be able to rise to this inspiration.

What will become of this world is up to us. And we can choose how we want to live. We are mistaken if we think this world is all of reality and it does not matter if we continue to live in a way that does not sustain and nurture us. We are not now, nor have we ever been, alone in the universe. We are part of a vast creation of intelligent life, one planet among many different kinds of inhabited worlds housing many levels of physical and spiritual levels of existence. Now, in this phase of our planetary evolution, the time has arrived for humans to begin to understand the greater context of universal reality and how it is orchestrated by the spirit presence of God. We have reached the point of intellectual comprehension and spiritual receptivity necessary to be enlightened by greater truths of reality.

We live in a universe created by a Divine Being, who as Jesus, appeared on this world to reveal a Divine Parent of love and compassion to all of his children of this world, not to just one religious tradition or racial group. Jesus' human life was the gift to lead all people to find God and to enjoy life more fully. Spirit has given us the keys to life, to the purpose and meaning of living. Now we must do the work ourselves to obtain the happiness we crave. This upliftment effort is our call to join the universal family. No longer are we to be downcast by fear; God's love transforms all fear into courage and power. Nor do we have to flounder aimlessly, for we have been given the pilot to guide us godward. No longer must we languish in monotony, for we have been given the keys to great creativity of self-expression. No longer should we feel neglected, for God is always by our side. Jesus has promised to return to this world, but first we must do the work. We must transform this world into the place where God lives in the hearts and minds of all people.

There is so much more I would like to convey, but each of you now has the tools and guidance contained in these pages to reach self-fulfillment with the help of your own indwelling spirit. What I would like to assure you is: You can achieve great happiness and love if you really want it – by starting your own relationship with God. Where it will lead you, only you and God know.

How much happiness do you want? How much adventure do you crave? Some people will seek skydiving, mountain climbing, or feats of athletic endurance, focusing on the adventures of the outer, physical world. What you are about to embark on is the adventure of finding your true self. This is the greatest adventure of life. For me, the inner adventure has proved more challenging, more exciting, because I have had to cast off fear and boldly go where I had not ventured before in discovering the depths of my personality gifts.

This journey is not for the faint-hearted, but it worth every ounce of effort. Until now, you may have been afraid to face up to your true self, afraid to face anxiety and fear that may have caused you great pain. With God, however, it is possible to become totally free from everything that has kept you bound in misery. Would you like this to happen to you?

We cannot expect others to assume the responsibility of planetary transformation. If each of us expects everyone else to be responsible, nothing will ever change. All of us share equally in the responsibility of correcting this world. Each individual has his or her own role to play. You can discover what your role is by developing your relationship with God. Listening to your spirit's loving personal message will tell you what God's plan is for you and help you to transform yourself and help the world.

This world *will* be healed. The healing has already begun. This is a promise our Creator Spirit has made to this world. Are you ready to participate in this monumental undertaking? Never before in the history of this planet has there been a time when so much spiritual power has been poured over the earth. Do you want to play a role in this epochal transformation? How much do you want your life and your planet to be freed from hopelessness and hate? If your answer is an unequivocal willingness to participate, God will be right there to help you. Seek the stillness and feel God's love. Depend upon God. Pray for others. Forgive yourself and your brothers and sisters. See the presence of the spirit in others. Practice this on a daily basis and you will be doing your part toward planetary transformation.

Above all, know that you are not alone. When you ask Spirit for spiritual healing and planetary transformation, trust that the help will be there. You may be unaware of its nature or its origin, but it will be there. You will not be disappointed in this; never will God fail you. You are loved. Always will our loving Creator and universal spiritual forces be there to uphold, uplift, and sustain you. Just take that first step of faith.

Your Creator is with you. Feel God's presence. Take as much of His love as you need to help you face the struggles as you grow in your awareness of cosmic reality. You cannot fail in this, for you have perfect divine love and strength at your side. Your goodness will attract the hungry souls who are seeking compassion. Your beauty will shine with the radiance of divine love. Your truth will inspire the sincere seeker.

The universe is calling you. Answer the call. Unlock the spirit within. Unlock God's love, the love you were born to live. Embrace your destiny!

Introducing:
The *Come into the Stillness* CD

The experience of God consciousness is as important to the spiritual growth process as learning new ideas about who and what God is. The meditation CD *Come into the Stillness* is a companion to the teachings in this book that will assist you in the practice of "stillness," an easy-to-follow seven-step meditation.

The seven steps will take you on an experiential journey to commune with your Inner Spirit, assisting you to recognize the voice of God within. You are guided to relax your body, quiet your mind, and elevate your awareness so the divine voice can be discerned. An introduction is followed by a guided meditation that takes you from step to step, with helpful suggestions and an opportunity for you to have your own experience during each step.

This valuable tool for your journey will help you to reorient your inner life and will expand your capacity to receive your own guidance for the magnificent journey with God.

To order the CD, and for further information, contact:
Center for Christ Consciousness
www.ctrforchristcon.org/materials.asp

Center for Christ Consciousness

From these teachings, a personal calling has been born that is fulfillment of my life's purpose. A fervor swelling within me has opened the way for me to share the love of God with all who want to deepen their personal relationship with their inner spirit and be free of the hurtful or confused wounds of the past. This is the call to ministry.

This ministry is the Center for Christ Consciousness. Its mission is to help people develop their personal relationship with God. The two major focuses are the practice of stillness – quieting the mind so the spirit of God within can be discerned – and healing: removing the impediments of fear, doubt, and diseases of the mind and body so the spirit of God within can communicate to your being.

A wide range of programs and materials are offered to enhance your spiritual growth and healing. Further teaching from the celestial teachers and our Divine Mother and Father are available on the website. Please also explore our video and audio presentations which are relevant to daily life situations and contain meditative experiences for your spiritual edification. The CCC provides a place of peace, receptivity, and acceptance for where you are in your path, and our beloved Creator guides you through love to heal and to foster your growth. May you find this to be a home for enlightenment and fulfillment. I thank Spirit for this opportunity to share these teachings with you, and hope they have benefited you. God bless you, dear reader, and illuminate the way for your light to shine.

INDEX

CPSIA information can be obtained at www.ICGtesting.com
Printed in the USA
LVOW101602090612

285273LV00001B/17/P